AUTHOR

Luigi Manes was born in Milan on 18 July 1966 and holds a degree in Business Economics. He has always been interested in the history of the Second World War, and in 2018 he published his first book, "Italia 43-45 - I mezzi delle unità cobelligeranti" (Mattioli 1885), written four hands with Paolo Crippa, followed shortly afterwards by "Carri armati Sherman in Sicilia" (Edizioni Ardite), produced together with Lorenzo Bovi. With Soldiershop he has published the following volumes: 'The Sherman medium tank in the European theatre of war' (2019), 'British tanks in the Second World War' (2019), 'Yugoslav armoured units 1940-1945' (2020, written with Paolo Crippa), 'The Legnano Combat Group' (2021) and 'Partisan tanks' (2022, with Paolo Crippa). He has also written several articles for the military modelling magazine 'Steel Art' and for the website 'Modellismo Più'. A football enthusiast, he is a big Inter Milan fan.

PUBLISHING'S NOTES

None of unpublished images or text of our book may be reproduced in any format without the expressed written permission of Luca Cristini Editore (already Soldiershop.com) when not indicate as marked with license creative commons 3.0 or 4.0. Luca Cristini Editore has made every reasonable effort to locate, contact and acknowledge rights holders and to correctly apply terms and conditions to Content.

Every effort has been made to trace the copyright of all the photographs. If there are unintentional omissions, please contact the publisher in writing at: info@soldiershop.com, who will correct all subsequent editions.

Our trademark: Luca Cristini Editore©, and the names of our series & brand: Soldiershop, Witness to war, Museum book, Bookmoon, Soldiers&Weapons, Battlefield, War in colour, Historical Biographies, Darwin's view, Fabula, Altrastoria, Italia Storica Ebook, Witness To History, Soldiers, Weapons & Uniforms, Storia etc. are herein © by Luca Cristini Editore.

LICENSES COMMONS

This book may utilize part of material marked with license creative commons 3.0 or 4.0 (CC BY 4.0), (CC BY-ND 4.0), (CC BY-SA 4.0) or (CC0 1.0). We give appropriate attribution credit and indicate if change were made in the acknowledgments field. Our WTW books series utilize only fonts licensed under the SIL Open Font License or other free use license.

For a complete list of Soldiershop titles please contact Luca Cristini Editore on our website: www.soldiershop.com or www.cristinieditore.com. E-mail: info@soldiershop.com

Title: **ALBANIAN UNITS IN THE SECOND WORLD WAR** Code.: **WTW-051 EN** By Luigi Manes
ISBN code: 9788893277495 first edition November 2023
Language: English. Size: 177,8x254mm Cover & Art Design: Luca S. Cristini

WITNESS TO WAR (SOLDIERSHOP) is a trademark of Luca Cristini Editore, via Orio, 35/4 - 24050 Zanica (BG) ITALY.

WITNESS TO WAR

ALBANIAN UNITS IN THE SECOND WORLD WAR

PHOTOS & IMAGES FROM WORLD WARTIME ARCHIVES

LUIGI MANES

BOOKS TO COLLECT

CONTENTS

Albania from the declaration of independence of 1912 to the reign of Zog I .... pag. 5

Operation Oltre Mare Tirana - The forces in the field .... pag. 9

The Italian occupation of Albania .... pag. 19

The Union between Italy and Albania .... pag. 20

The Albanian units of the Royal Italian Army .... pag. 21

The Albanian Fascist Militia .... pag. 43

Reconstitution and employment of the Albanian Army after the Armistice .... pag. 51

The Albanians in the Waffen – SS .... pag. 59

Resistance and civil war .... pag. 71

The Albanian National Liberation Army .... pag. 77

Italian soldiers in Albanian resistance .... pag. 94

Bibliography .... pag. 97

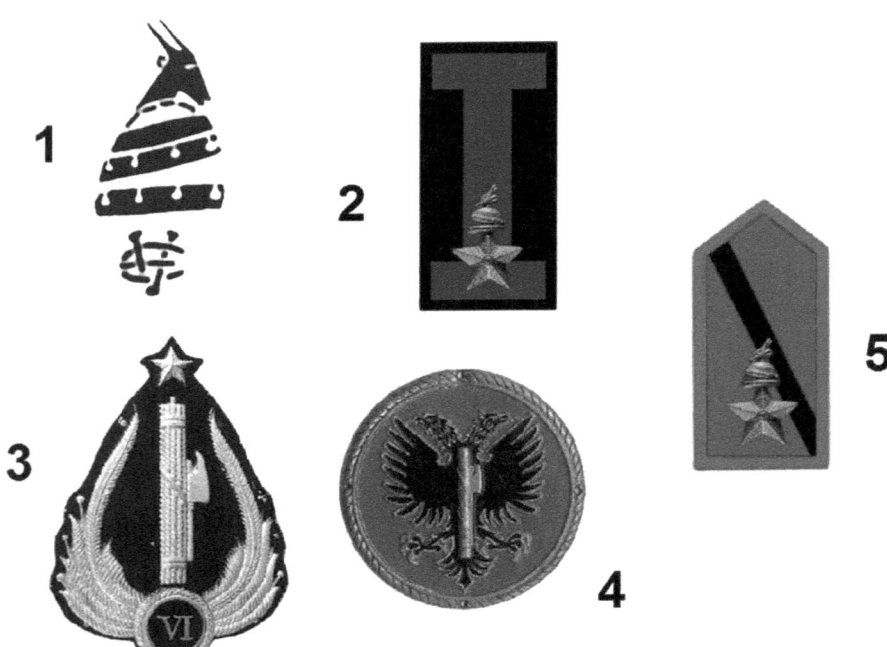

1. M33 helmet frieze of the *"Royal Albanian Guard"*.
2. Collar patch for officers of the *"Royal Albanian Guard"*. Note the typical knurling on the star surface.
3. M.V.S.N. frieze applied on the cap adopted by the *"Albanian Fascist Militia"*.
4. Circular humeral badge of the *"Albanian Fascist Militia"*.
5. Pentagonal collar patch for officers of the *"Albanian Rifle"* regiments. Note the typical knurling on the star surface.

ALBANIA FROM THE DECLARATION OF INDEPENDENCE OF 1912 TO THE REIGN OF ZOG I HISTORICAL BACKGROUND

On 28 November 1912 the Albanian National Congress, chaired by Ismail Qemali[1], proclaimed the independence of the "Land of Eagles", effectively ending the Turkish domination which began in 1385. After the Balkan Wars which involved a reconfiguration of the territorial structures of the belligerent nations, the borders of the new State were defined and according to what established by the great European powers, the German Prince William of Wied became Prince of Albania in April 1914. At the outbreak of the First World War, Austria-Hungary tried in vain to convince William to side with the Central Powers. Unable to accept the requests of the Albanian people and the leaders of the local communities, isolated internally and without connections abroad, the sovereign was forced to abandon the country. On 3 September 1914 William of Wied left Durrës on board the Italian ship *"Misurata"*, bound for Venice, to return to Germany. Thus ended the short reign of the German Protestant Prince who had been chosen to lead subjects belonging to three different confessions: the Muslim one, predominant and introduced by the Ottomans, the Orthodox Christian one and the Catholic one. Power was assumed by Essad Pasha Toptani, former Albanian Member of the Ottoman parliament and military leader during the First Balkan War, subsequently appointed Minister of War and Minister of the Interior by William. Toptani, who returned to his homeland after taking refuge in Italy to escape accusations of having plotted against the Prince, was elected Prime Minister in October 1914 and, supported by the Serbs, placed Albania against the Central Powers. The Albanian territory, which had become a theater of war, was consequently occupied by Austro-Hungarian, Serbian, Montenegrin, Greek, French and Italian troops, the latter present in the country since the autumn of 1914. Although on 4 June 1917 with a clever move Italy reaffirmed integrity and independence of Albania, at the end of the Great War the "Land of Eagles" ran the risk of being dismembered to satisfy the appetites of its neighbors. In fact, Serbia longed for an access to the sea, while Greece had instead set its sights on the southern Albanian regions. Such a perspective could not be endorsed by the Italian government which also entered into conflict with the Entente Powers on other issues, including that of Fiume. In 1919, thanks to an agreement with Greece[2], Rome was able to maintain control over the Straits of Otranto by retaining possession of Sazan Island and confirming sovereignty over Vlorë, a city which however returned to the "Land of Eagles" in 1920. In 1921, at the Paris Conference, Italy assumed the role of guarantor of the independence of Albania which was also admitted to the League of Nations. With the fall of the Austro-Hungarian and Ottoman empires, the strengthening of the small Balkan State was considered by Italy to be a crucial factor for the protection of its interests in the Adriatic. In that same period the figure of Ahmet Zog emerged[3], destined to mark the Albanian political landscape until 1939. Representative of the class of large landowners and former Minister of the Interior in the government of

---

[1] Ismail Qemali was born in Vlorë in 1844. He is considered to be the founder of the Albanian State. He died in Perugia (Italy) in 1919.
[2] Italy had obtained possession of Sazan Island and Vlorë with the London Pact of 26 April 1915.
[3] Ahmet Zogolli, better known as Zog, was born in 1895. Member of a family of landowners from Mathi, a region in northern Albania, he attended the Military Academy of Constantinople. After the Balkan Wars, with Albania under the dominion of Vienna, he joined the Austrian army and reached the rank of colonel. In conjunction with his appointment as Prime Minister (24 December 1922) he decided to do without the name of Turkish origin, Ahmet, and called himself simply Zog. In 1925 he was elected President of the newly proclaimed Albanian Republic. He managed to be crowned King of Albania on 1 September 1928.

Sulejman Delvina[4], formed in 1920 following the Congress of Lushnjë with which Albanian political exponents affirmed their desire to safeguard the autonomy of the nation, Zog became Prime Minister on 24 December 1922. Soon the new head of government had to deal with the fierce opposition of the political group led by Fan Noli, Orthodox bishop of Durrës, allied with the democratic nationalist faction and with the Committee for the National Defence of Kosovo which aspired to the liberation of the territory controlled by Serbia and inhabited mostly by ethnic Albanian population. Not only did the opponents accuse Zog of failing to implement the agrarian reform but they also pushed for justice and public administration reform and for the State to take over the exploitation of national oil resources, at the time sole prerogative of important foreign companies such as the American Standard Oil and the Anglo-Persian Oil Company. In 1924 the harsh political conflict turned into an armed struggle which caused the defenestration of Zog who was replaced as Prime Minister by Shefqet Vërlaci[5]. After the formation of a new executive by Noli, Zog fled to Yugoslavia where he was welcomed by Serbian nationalists, opposed to the claims advanced by the Committee for the National Defence of Kosovo. The situation reversed during the last month of the year. On 13 December 1924 the "Zogist" militias supported by Yugoslav artillery units entered Albania and on 24 December they reached Tiranë. On 19 January 1925, after the dissolution of the movements that opposed Zog, the birth of the Republic of Albania was proclaimed. Having rewarded Yugoslavia with some border changes for the support provided, Zog, who became President of the Albanian Republic, worked to consolidate the privileges enjoyed in the country by foreign oil companies and encouraged the entry of foreign capitals through the granting of advantageous tax breaks. Zog's rapprochement with Italy also dates back to that time, motivated by the need to counterbalance Belgrade's influence on Tiranë and seized by Mussolini as a chance to begin a series of economic and military interventions in Albania. Since 1925 secret agreements developed between Italy and Albania, above all thanks to the work of the Member of the Italian Parliament Alessandro Lessona[6]. On 27 November 1926, a friendship and security pact was signed in Tiranë, welcomed with satisfaction by both parties: Mussolini believed that a strong bond with Albania was indispensable for Italy's security, Zog wished to create a military alliance capable of discourage any Greek and Yugoslavian expansionist aims. One year later the pact was perfected in a twenty-five-year defensive alliance treaty (Treaty of Tiranë) which, although it satisfied the aspiration of the Shqiptar Prime Minister to become King with the name of Zog I, transformed Albania into a satellite State of Italy. At the beginning of the 1930s, nationalist upheavals led the sovereign to review his foreign policy approach, considered too accommodating towards the Italian government by a segment of Albanian public opinion. The cooling of relations with Tiranë pushed Rome to react with the suspension of the disbursement of an important loan granted in 1931 in view of the confirmation of the agreements stipulated in previous years. The King of Albania responded in turn with measures such as the introduction of a public education system which penalized Italian Catholic private schools and the

---

4 At the end of 1920 the executive led by Delvina resigned and gave way to a government presided over by Iljaz Vrioni, one of the signatories of the Albanian Declaration of Independence of 28 November 1912. Subsequently Sulejman Delvina opposed Zog's power.
5 Shefqet Vërlaci supported Zog's appointment as Prime Minister. On 12 April 1939, with the annexation of Albania to Italy, Vërlaci became head of the Albanian government, holding the position until 3 December 1941. He was also appointed Senator of Kingdom of Italy.
6 In the military field, the Kingdom of Albania made its territory available to Italy in the event of a conflict against Yugoslavia. Of great importance in economic terms were the concession of agricultural areas and the permits for the exploitation of oil areas in the Devoli region, granted to the Azienda Italiana Petroli Albania (AIPA, later absorbed by AGIP as a result of an Italian law of 1940), managed by the Italian State Railways, the birth of the Society for the Economic Development of Albania (Società per lo Sviluppo Economico dell'Albania, SVEA) in April 1925 to finance the fulfilment of public works through the participation of Italian companies and the establishment of an Albanian central bank, the National Bank of Albania, mostly with Italian capital in September 1925. Totally controlled by Italy, the Albanian credit institution had its registered office in Rome and was both an issuing and commercial bank.

failure to renew the positions granted to Italian military advisors and instructors which also resulted in the removal of the Royal Italian Army General Alberto Pariani, head of the Italian military mission to the Albanian Armed Forces. Zog, however, was not able to give up vital economic aid from Rome and after having unsuccessfully tried to get closer to France in order to free himself to some extent from Italian pressure, he could only retrace his steps. Thanks to Albania's failure to adhere to the sanctions imposed on Italy by the League of Nations for the conflict in Ethiopia, Zog obtained new loans from Rome aimed at investments in the agricultural and military spheres. The systematic recourse to foreign loans, which became necessary in the absence of a credible program for the recovery of public finances, consolidated Italy's primacy over the Albanian economy. A timid attempt to modernize the State's administrative apparatus, accompanied by liberal measures which made possible the formation of trade unions to protect workers in the mining sector and granted greater freedom of the press, was initiated by the executive led by Mehdi Frashëri, a pro-Italian personality, appointed Prime Minister by the Albanian King in 1935. In the following years, events such as the Spanish War and the annexation of Austria by Germany shocked Europe, relegating Albania to the background. After the Munich Conference (1938) which sanctioned the annexation of the Sudetenland to Germany, the fate of Zog's Kingdom was entirely left at the mercy of Italy.

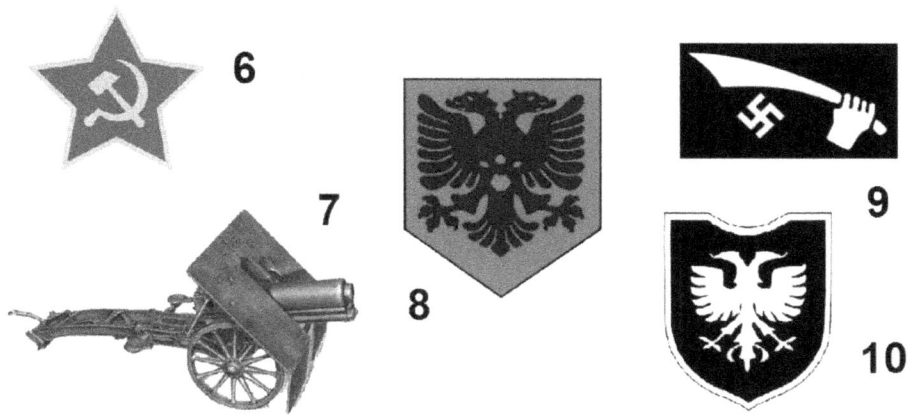

6. Cap frieze of the Albanian National Liberation Army.
7. 75/13 pack howitzer.
8. Cap frieze of the *Balli Kombëtar*.
9. Collar tab of the 13. Waffen – Gebirgs – Division der SS *"Handschar"*.
10. Insignia of the 21. Waffen – Gebirgs – Division der SS *"Skanderbeg"*.

▲ The territory of Albania between 1939 and 1944.

OPERATION OLTRE MARE TIRANA
THE FORCES IN THE FIELD

At the end of the 1930s, despite the conclusion of further agreements on economic and commercial matters, the stability of political relations between Rome and Tiranë began to creak. Not only was Zog opposed by young people, especially by those who, having studied abroad, had been able to see for themselves how distant the reality of their country was from that of the rest of Europe, but he was also disliked by the most advanced part of Albanian society which saw the promises of economic and civil development unfulfilled. The position of the sovereign, hostile to any serious reform measure and mainly concerned with strengthening his own power, quickly became precarious. The possibility that Zog could turn to other powers to remain firmly in the saddle, perhaps to Germany that had just seized Prague, Bohemia and Moravia, persuaded the Duce to implement a plan for the invasion of Albania, strongly favoured by the Minister of Foreign Affairs Galeazzo Ciano[7]. The rejection of proposals illustrated in an ultimatum[8] addressed to the Albanian King by the Italian government would have given the green light to the invasion. With Zog's refusal, Operation Oltre Mare Tirana (O.M.T.) began on 7 April 1939. The Italian Expeditionary Force, made up of approximately 22,000 men under the orders of General Alfredo Guzzoni, was divided into three echelons and obtained the support of air and naval forces. The first echelon, the only one to participate in the fighting since the others[9] arrived in Albanian territory when it was over, was structured on four columns:

Column of Durrës (General Giovanni Messe)

- One Bersaglieri regiment (Colonel Sozzani) with a Bersaglieri regimental command (2nd) and three Bersaglieri battalions (II/2, XVII/2 and XIV/5)
- One Bersaglieri tactical group (Colonel Anderson) on two Bersaglieri battalions (X/7 and XXVII/11)
- A Light Tank Group (Colonel D'Antoni) composed of two L Tank battalions (VIII and X, both from the 31st Tank Infantry Regiment)
- One battalion (I/47) of the *"Murge"* Infantry Division
- A 20 mm battery of the *"Murge"* Infantry Division

---

7 Ciano influenced Mussolini's opinion regarding the opportunity of the operation by highlighting the most important factors that in his opinion played in favor of such a decision: the sympathies enjoyed by the Italians in the ranks of Zog's armed forces, the disconnect between Albanian regime and Albanian citizens who would have welcomed the Italians as liberators, the acquiescence of Yugoslavia and, particularly, the concern that the Germans could anticipate Italy's initiatives and give rise to a project of expansion in the Balkans.
8 The definitive version of the ultimatum sent to Zog included the following points: 1) in the event that the country found itself in danger, Albanian roads, ports and airports had to be made available to Italy; 2) the presence of an Italian deputy minister had to be guaranteed in all ministries of the Albanian government; 3) Italian citizens in Albania were to be granted the enjoyment of the civil and political rights typical of Albanian citizens; 4) the Italian legation in Tiranë and the Albanian legation in Rome were to be transformed into embassies. If the answer was yes, the two countries would have signed a new treaty.
9 The first echelon had a total strength of over 13,000 men. The second echelon was made up of an Infantry battalion (II/47 of the *"Murge"* Division, in addition to the command of the 47th Infantry Regiment and the 65/17 battery of the same regiment), a Machine Gun battalion (IX Army Corps Machine Gun Battalion), two Cavalry Squadron Groups (I/*"Lancieri di Aosta"* and II/*"Genova Cavalleria"*), three artillery groups (IV 100/17 Group of the 14th Artillery Regiment *"Murge"*, XVIII 105/28 Army Corps Group and 149/13 CXV Army Corps Group), a garrison company, a bridge company, an engineer company, various services. The third echelon included a large part of the *"Murge"* Infantry Division (except the units assigned to the second echelon), a Blackshirts (CC.NN., Camicie Nere) battalion (XCII), various services. A Blackshirts Battalion Group also landed (CXI, CXII, CLII), under the command of Consul Peano.

- A 65/17 support battery of the 3rd Granatieri (Grenadier) Regiment
- A light vehicle section and various Signal units (radio operators and radio stations sections)

Column of Shëngjin (Colonel Arturo Scattini)

- A Bersaglieri regimental command (9th) with three Bersaglieri battalions (VI/6, III/8 and XXVIII/9)
- Two companies of the *"San Marco"* Marine Battalion (Royal Italian Navy)
- A heavy vehicle section and various Signal units (radio operators and radio stations sections)

Column of Vlorë (Colonel Tullio Bernardi)

- A Bersaglieri regimental command (1st) with two Bersaglieri cyclist battalions (I/1 and XVI/10)
- Blackshirts Battalion Group (Consul Nannini) with two Blackshirts battalions (XL and LXXVI)
- A heavy vehicle section and various Signal units (radio stations)

Column of Sarandë (Colonel Mario Carasi)

- One Bersaglieri regimental command (12th) with two Bersaglieri cyclist battalions (XX/3 and XXIII/12)
- III Fast Tank Group *"San Giorgio"*
- Two companies of the *"San Marco"* Marine Battalion (Royal Italian Navy)
- A heavy vehicle section, a mechanical workshop and various Signal units (radio operators and radio stations sections)

At the time of the Italian invasion, King Zog I held supreme command of the Albanian armed forces, better known as the Royal Albanian Army (*"Ushtria Mbretërore Shqiptare"*). General Xhemal Aranitasi was Commander of the Army, the Austrian noble-birth General Gustav von Myrdacz, since the 1920s in charge of the organization of the Albanian military apparatus, was Chief of the General Staff. At the end of the 1930s around 15,000 men were probably in actual service in Zog's army but a more reliable figure would be around 8,000 - 10,000 mobilized soldiers, of which 450 - 500 officers and 700 - 800 non-commissioned officers, excluding Gendarmerie and Border Guard units[10], which were organized as follows:

Infantry

At the beginning of 1939 the Albanian Infantry had seven battalions in its ranks. These units had been named after some of the most famous peaks of the "Land of Eagles": *"Tarabosh"* (recruitment center in Shkodër), *"Korata"*, *"Deja"*, *"Dajti"* (all three with recruitment center in Tiranë), *"Kaptina"* (recruitment center in Elbasan), *"Tomori"* (recruitment center in Berat), *"Gramos"* (recruitment center in Korça)[11]. Each battalion consisted, on paper, of Headquarters (about 20 men), three rifle

---

[10] Starting from the mid-1920s, many Albanians were able to access Italian Military Schools. On the immediate eve of Operation Oltre Mare Tirana, 61 of them were training at the Military Academies of Italy. Zog's nephew was at the Specialist School of the Royal Italian Air Force.
[11] Overall, the Albanian Infantry should have consisted of nine battalions but at the time of the Italian invasion only seven

companies (each with at least 120 men, on a company Headquarters and 3 platoons divided into 3 squads), a machine gun company (on 3 platoons), various services. The *"Tarabosh"*, *"Kaptina"*, *"Tomori"* and *"Gramos"* battalions were understrength units, having only two rifle companies and one machine gun company on two platoons.

Artillery

The Albanian Artillery included eight 65/17 batteries (each on 2 pieces), four 75/13 batteries (each on 2 Skoda 75/13 pack howitzers), two 75/27 field batteries, one horse-drawn, the other officially transported by trucks (both on 4 75/27 model 1906 guns). A third 75/27 battery equipped with 4 guns (apparently housed within fortified emplacements built by Italian engineers) defended the port of Durrës[12]. Three small caliber anti-aircraft batteries, each with 6 machine guns (probably 8 mm Schwarzlose M07/12 machine guns mounted on anti-aircraft carriages and given to the Albanians by the Italians), were located in Shëngjin, Durrës and Sarandë. Various sources also mention the existence of an artillery unit at the divisional level, directly dependent on the High Command of the Albanian Army, which included a 75/13 group (on 3 batteries, each with 2 pack howitzers) and a 75/27 group (on 2 batteries of 4 pieces, one horse-drawn, the other truck-transported)[13]. As will be seen, there were also two further 75/13 batteries (each provided with 4 pieces), one (horse-drawn) belonged to the Gendarmerie, the other (presumably not horse-drawn) was in service with the Royal Guard[14].

Engineer Corps

In 1939, three sapper-miner companies (each with a Headquarters and three platoons), a bridge section and a radiotelegraph and telephone operators company were operational within the Engineer Corps. The radiotelegraph and telephone operators company fulfilled the needs of the entire Army and was composed of company Headquarters (with 1 truck), a radiotelegraph section (with 1 car, 3 horses, 6 R3 radiotelegraph stations, 2 R5 radiotelegraph stations), a telephone operators section and a photo electrician section (with 4 horses). The creation of support companies was also envisaged, each on Headquarters (1 car and 1 horse), Transport Detachment (with 24 horses and a variable number of carts), Pack Train, Logistics Detachment (with 1 truck and several horses).

Gendarmerie

The Gendarmerie was responsible for maintaining public order but also had to contribute to the defense of the country. From 1931 to 1939 it was commanded by Colonel Shefki Shatku[15]. Unlike the rest of the army, British instructors were present in the Gendarmerie. This allowed Zog to counterbalance to some extent the considerable weight of the Italian military mission with the Albanian Armed Forces. The greater willingness to resist the Italian invasion shown by certain formations under Colonel Shatku could partially be explained by the influence exercised on the Gendarmes by the instructors from across the Channel. At the highest hierarchical level the Albanian commander was supported by General Jocelyn Percy, in turn assisted by General George H.M. Richey. The Gendarmerie was made up of six battalions which were based in Gjirokastër (600 men), Berat (500

---

had been formed. The incomplete battalions had a strength of less than 500 men.
12 Worthy of note is the presence in Durrës of two old forts built by the Turks which, since 1912, housed three pieces of light artillery (of unknown caliber). However, it is not clear whether these artilleries were still in place in April 1939.
13 However, it cannot be ruled out that these were batteries already in place, grouped into a unit directly at the orders of Albanian Army High Command.
14 Mountain gun batteries bore the names of important Albanian rivers: Mathi, Drin, Semani and Vjosë (Voiussa).
15 Shefki Shatku was promoted to colonel on 28 November 1938. He collected various awards including the Iron Cross 2nd Class, received from the Kaiser. In 1933 he was awarded Commander of the Order of Skanderbeg by Zog and in 1937 he was decorated with the medal of Grand Officer of the Order of the Crown of Italy by King Victor Emmanuel III.

men), Elbasan (400 men), Shkodër (400 men), Durrës (500 men), Kukës (400 men). Each battalion was also equipped with 4 Schwarzlose M07/12 machine guns. A training battalion (600 men) provided with a 75/13 battery on 4 pieces and 12 Fiat 14/35 machine guns[16] was stationed in Burreli. The Gendarmerie had on paper a strength of 3,782 men, of which 136 officers but Italian sources report a total of 2,867 gendarmes, given by 131 officers and 2,736 non-commissioned officers and troops.

Border Guard

In 1925 a group of officers from the Italian Guardia di Finanza (customs police) received the task of organizing the Albanian Border Guard. Its duties consisted of protecting national borders from foreign interference and repressing smuggling activities. The Border Guard was composed of four battalions stationed in Delvinë, Durrës, Shkodër and Korça where a training battalion was also based. In the first months of 1939 the overall strength of the Albanian Border Guard was probably made up of 91 officers, 222 non-commissioned officers and 1,500 soldiers, distributed across 14 companies, 48 platoons and 119 squads.

Royal Guard

Commanded by Colonel Hysen Selmani, in April 1939 the Royal Guard had a strength of 926 men including officers, non-commissioned officers and troops. It was made up of an Honor Guard Company assigned to representation services, an Infantry Battalion on Headquarters and 4 rifle companies, an artillery battery (with 4 75/13 pack howitzers, 152 men of which 4 officers and also 59 horses), a Cavalry Squadron (with 70 – 90 men, the only one of its type in the Albanian army which lacked other Cavalry units), Royal Band and Depot. The Infantry Battalion consisted of approximately 600 Guards. The Royal Guard was responsible for protecting the King from any type of aggression.

Vehicle Park

The Vehicle Park was based in Tiranë and included Headquarters, Materials Depot, Fuel Depot, Mechanical Workshops and Driving School. Overall, around 600 drivers were available for the Army's disparate needs. In 1936 the vehicle fleet included 200 cars and light trucks, 300 2 and 3 ton trucks and 20 buses. More precisely, among the vehicles in service there were various Italian models such as the Fiat 521, 521C and 525 cars and the Fiat 15-ter trucks as well as a limited number of Ford cars and Fordson light trucks, vehicles assembled under license in Romania.

Tank and Armored Car Squadron

The Vehicle Park also oversaw a small armored unit stationed in Tiranë, the Tank and Armored Car Squadron, which in 1939 almost certainly had at least 2 Fiat 3000 light tanks (armed with machine guns and sold by the Italians in the 1930s) and 6 L3 fast tanks (apparently all CV33s). The equipment was completed by 6 Lancia 1ZM armored cars and an indeterminate but limited quantity of Bianchi armored cars. Several doubts remain about the real consistency of this tiny formation because it is not clear how many armored vehicles were in good condition at the beginning of 1939.

Medical Service

Medical Service personnel were attached to the most important units. Four Military Hospitals (presumably based in Shkodër, Sarandë, Tiranë and Vlorë) met the needs of the entire Albanian Army. A veterinary service was also available.

---

16 The Gendarmerie School was transferred from Durrës to Burreli at the beginning of May 1935.

Reserve

In the Albanian Army the reserves were made up of volunteers. In 1939 there were approximately 8,000 men in battalions based in ten prefectures (Vlorë, Berat, Peshkopi, Durrës, Elbasan, Gjirokastër, Korça, Kukës, Shkodër, Tiranë). The Reserve battalions had 2 or 3 infantry companies and sometimes also included a machine gun company. These units were supposed to carry out auxiliary functions, especially in the rear, although some of them drew personnel who were directly sent to replenish undersized units intended to operate on the front-line. In addition to these uniformed volunteers there were militias known as *Shuma* (multitudes), established in mountainous and rural areas. Overall there were 30,000 fighters in civilian clothes, in some cases dressed in the typical costumes of the regions of origin, equipped with various armaments including Vetterli Vitali rifles and old muzzle-loading muskets dating back to the period of Turkish rule. The rank of the 1,200 *Shuma* officers was considered lower than that of platoon commander in the regular army.

Women's Battalions

Several young women from Tiranë and the surrounding region were enrolled in three women's battalions named after Zog's three sisters: Myzejen, Ruhije and Maxhide. These units, however, had no military potential since the activities practiced by the girls who were part of them consisted exclusively of performing gymnastic exercises or parading dressed in uniform.

Air Force

In the imminence of the Operation Oltre Mare Tirana, Albania probably did not have any aircraft suitable to be used for military purposes. However, it is not possible to exclude the presence of at least a couple of the 5 German-made Albatros C.XV/L47 reconnaissance aircraft acquired in the 1920s, used essentially for training activities.

Navy

Around 1938 the Albanian Navy consisted of nearly 160 sailors, including 17 officers. Four port authorities were based in Shëngjin, Durrës, Vlorë and Sarandë. In the 1930s, in addition to a *"flotilla"* of 4 M.A.S. (Motoscafo Armato Silurante) torpedo boats obtained from Italy and named *"Durrës"*, *"Sarandë"*, *"Tiranë"* and *"Vlorë"*, the Navy was also equipped with two gunboats, named *"Shqipnija"* and *"Skënderbeu"*[17], both originally German minesweepers. The first was in fact a *Flachgehendeminensuchboote 16*, the second a *Flachgehendeminensuchboote 23*. Inefficient since 1935, the two ships did not return to active service in the following years. In 1939, even the M.A.S. were no longer able to go to sea and as a consequence of this situation, part of the crews of the Albanian vessels were reorganized into a Marine Infantry Platoon.

---

[17] Gjergj Kastrioti also known as Scanderbeg or Skënderbeu (1405 – 1468), from the Turkish Iskander (Alexander) and bey (title indicating the sovereigns of vassal states of the Ottoman Empire), is recognized as the greatest hero of the Albanian nation. After the Albanian territories governed by his father (Gjon I) were placed under the sovereignty of Sultan Murad II, Scanderbeg, forced to convert to Islam, joined the Ottoman army in which he quickly became one of the most daring leaders. Moved by an unquenched feeling of revenge, in 1443, on the occasion of the victory achieved over the Turks by a large army made up of Poles, Hungarians and Serbs led by János Hunyadi at Niš, he left the Sultan's camp to return to Albania. Once the city of Kruja was liberated from the Ottomans, Scanderbeg re-embraced the Christian faith and became commander of an army of Albanian princes united in the League of Lezhë. The successes achieved against the Turks from 1444 to 1447 contributed to spreading his fame to the rest of Europe. After signing a peace agreement with Venice, he tried in vain to come to the aid of Hunyadi's troops, defeated at Kosovo Polje in 1448 at the hands of Murad II. In 1451 he established an alliance with Alfonso V of Aragon, King of Naples. From 1457 to 1458 he obtained other great victories against overwhelming Turkish forces. Pope Callixtus III gave him the nickname of Athleta Christi, recognizing him as a staunch defender of the Christian faith. In 1461 Scanderbeg went to Italy, to help Ferdinand I (son of Alfonso V), to fight against John of Anjou. From 1462 to 1467 he repeatedly defeated the Ottoman troops of Muhammad II. Struck by malaria, he died unconquered in the fortress of Lezhë just as Venice, worried about Turkish expansionism towards the heart of Europe, was about to offer him a proposal for an alliance.

Most of the forces described had been assigned to five operational zones or, more specifically, to four Military Zones and the Durrës Garrison. In 1939 the various units were deployed as follows:

Zone I (between the locality of Milot and the course of the Shkumbini River)

- *"Dajti"* Infantry Battalion
- *"Deja"* Infantry Battalion
- *"Korata"* Infantry Battalion
- Four 65/17 batteries
- A sappers – miners company
- A radiotelegraph station (R3)
- Reservists (1,000 men)

Zone II (between the locality of Milot and Shkodër)

- *"Gramos"* Infantry Battalion
- *"Tarabosh"* Infantry Battalion
- Two 65/17 batteries
- A Gendarmerie battalion
- A radiotelegraph station (R3)
- Reservists (500 men)

Zone III (between the courses of the Shkumbini and Vjosë rivers)

- *"Kaptina"* Infantry Battalion
- *"Tomori"* Infantry Battalion
- Two 65/17 batteries
- A Gendarmerie battalion
- A sappers – miners platoon
- A radiotelegraph station (R3)
- Reservists (unspecified number)

Zone IV (area around Sarandë)

- A Gendarmerie battalion
- Two Border Guard battalions
- A radiotelegraph station (R3)
- Reservists (800 men)

Durrës Garrison

- A Gendarmerie battalion
- A Border Guard battalion
- A 75/13 battery
- A 75/27 coastal battery
- A Marine Infantry platoon
- A sappers – miners company
- A radiotelegraph station (R3)
- Reservists (800 men)

All other units continued to depend on their respective superior commands. As regards individual and support weapons, the Albanian regular forces had just under 30,000 rifles at their disposal at the time (25,000 of Italian production, mainly Carcano, the remainder mostly Mannlicher - Schönauer) and around a hundred machine guns (mainly Fiat 14/35 and Schwarzlose M07/12).

▲ Soldiers from King Zog's army. Note the close resemblance of the Albanian uniforms to the Italian ones.

▲ An Albanian unit parades in front of Zog.

▼ Princess Myzejen at the head of the women's battalion that bears her name.

▲ Italian Foreign Minister Galeazzo Ciano reviews an Albanian infantry unit. On the left, General Xhemal Aranitasi, commander of the Army, on the right, Zog's Aide-de-Camp, Zef Sereqi. The latter was placed in the role of division general in permanent effective service in the Royal Italian Army after the annexation of Albania to Italy.

▼ The 75/27 truck-transported battery of the Albanian army. The vehicles appearing in this picture are Fiat 15-ter trucks.

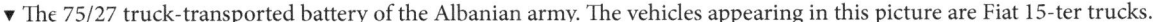

▲ An Albanian truck-transported artillery piece. It is almost certainly a 75/27 mod. 1906 gun belonging to the same battery depicted in the previous picture.

▼ The Albanian Royal Couple portrayed together with the King's three sisters. The Italian invasion forced Zog and his wife, the Hungarian Countess Géraldine Apponyi, into exile.

THE ITALIAN OCCUPATION OF ALBANIA

According to the Operation Oltre Mare Tirana order, the Italian columns of the first echelon were to land at dawn on 7 April 1939. The conquest of Tiranë was entrusted to the Column of Durrës. Once landed, the troops at the orders of General Messe had to neutralize a determined resistance put up by around 500 Albanian soldiers, mostly belonging to a Gendarmerie battalion, supported by a sappers - miners company and elements of the Marine Infantry Platoon deployed in the port city. Gendarmerie Major Abaz Kupi and Navy Petty Officer Mujo Ulqinaku stood out among the defenders in the fighting.[18]. The 1st battalion of the 47th Regiment of the *"Murge"* Infantry Division had been assigned the task of garrisoning Durrës in order to allow the troops of General Messe to launch themselves in the direction of the Albanian capital, where they would be joined by the Grenadier training regiment (formed with elements of the 3rd Granatieri Regiment) on two battalions (transported by air) commanded by Colonel Mannerini. General Messe's column entered Tiranë on 8 April in the morning. At *Shëngjin*, the two companies of the *"San Marco"* Battalion established an initial beachhead from which Colonel Scattini's other units were able to move towards the designated destinations, Lezhë and Shkodër. The advance of the XXVIII Bersaglieri Battalion on Lezhë, taken in the early hours of the afternoon on 7 April, was temporarily arrested by a formation of 150 Albanians. At 4.30 pm on 8 April the column's troops reached Shkodër. The two Blackshirts battalions (XL and LXXVI) assigned to Colonel Bernardi's contingent were responsible for initially ensuring control of Vlorë and subsequently that of Fier. The primary objective of Column of Vlorë was the occupation of the oil-producing area of the Devoli basin. The Italian landing was hindered by the action of elements of the Albanian Gendarmerie, immediately countered by the intervention of a destroyer and by the automatic weapons of Bersaglieri units. During the advance, the Blackshirts and the Bersaglieri got the better of the defenders in other clashes, first near Vlorë and later in the vicinity of Bestrovë. Colonel Carasi's column, tasked with taking over Delvinë and Gjirokastër, also benefited from the support of units belonging to the *"San Marco"* Battalion for the capture of the port of Sarandë, city defended by elements of the Gendarmerie. Having noted the impossibility of resisting from the beginning of the invasion, King Zog, Queen Géraldine and their first-born Leka (born only two days earlier) fled to Greece and then found asylum in Great Britain. In the space of seventy-two hours, the Italian forces managed to occupy all the intended objectives. On 13 April 1939 the Italian Expeditionary Force was renamed Army Corps Command of Albania (Comando Corpo d'Armata d'Albania).

---

18 A monument built in Durrës commemorates the figure of Mujo Ulqinaku, who fell in the clashes of 7 April 1939.

THE UNION BETWEEN ITALY AND ALBANIA

The Italian occupation inaugurated a new historical phase in the relations between the two shores of the Adriatic Sea, linked by numerous common events over the previous centuries. In conjunction with the advance of the Italian troops into Albanian territory, an interim Executive Committee was set up, chaired by Xhafer Ypi, a politician responsible for convening a Constituent Assembly which would ask Victor Emmanuel III to take the Crown of Albania. On 16 April 1939, with the formal consent of the Savoyard monarch, the "Land of Eagles" was annexed to Italy in the form of personal union. The executive power effectively passed to the Italian King who appointed Francesco Jacomoni di San Savino, former plenipotentiary of Italy in Tiranë, Lieutenant General of the Kingdom for the exercise of royal powers[19]. Shefqet Vërlaci was called to preside over the new Albanian Government[20]. On 18 April 1939 with Royal Decree n. 624 the Undersecretariat of State for Albanian Affairs was created, a body directly dependent on the Ministry of Foreign Affairs of Rome, at the head of which Zenone Benini was appointed. It was established that the citizens of the two states would be guaranteed the rights that they already enjoyed on their respective national territories. On 2 June 1939 the Albanian Fascist Party (Partia Fashiste Shqiptare) was founded, as a direct subsidiary of the National Fascist Party (Partito Nazionale Fascista). The organization of the Shqiptar political formation was identical to that of the Italian party and therefore also included an organization that took care of the military, physical and moral preparation of boys and girls from beyond the Adriatic Sea, the Albanian Lictor Youth (*Gioventù Albanese del Littorio*). The new Statute of the Kingdom of Albania[21], in force since 4 June 1939, sanctioned the establishment of the Supreme Fascist Corporate Council, modeled on the example of the Chamber of Fasces and Corporations. The new body replaced the suppressed Albanian Parliament but not having been endowed with legislative power, concentrated in the hands of the King, it exercised a mere consultative function. The annexation also had significant consequences in other fields. A customs union was created between the two countries and a fixed parity was established between the Albanian Franc and the Italian Lira. Economic activity received a further boost from the launch of a major public works program. There were numerous cultural and scientific initiatives promoted by the Italian Government in Albania. Albanian personalities became members of various Italian academies and universities. Young people, especially the most deserving, were able to go to study in Italy. Freedom of worship, protected by the Albanian Constitution of 1928, was maintained. This condition favored the sending of Catholic missions from Italy to a country that Ottoman domination had made predominantly Muslim. The union between the two States also brought about significant changes in the military sphere: on 13 July 1939, with law no. 1115, the Albanian armed forces were absorbed into the Italian ones and nine days later the High Command of Troops in Albania (Comando Superiore Truppe Albania) was created.

---

19 A regulation proposal text dating back to 14 April 1939, reaffirmed in law no. 580 promulgated on 16 April 1939 stated: "Art. 1 - The King of Italy, having accepted the Crown of Albania, assumes for himself and his successors the title of King of Italy and Albania, Emperor of Ethiopia. Art. 2 - The King of Italy and Albania, Emperor of Ethiopia, will be represented in Albania by a Lieutenant General, who will reside in Tiranë".
20 Shefqet Vërlaci and other Albanian political leaders such as Gjon Marka Gjoni, Mustafà Merlika Kruja and Vangjel Turtulli were appointed senators of the Kingdom of Italy in 1939.
21 The Fundamental Statute of the Kingdom of Albania reaffirmed the decision to take the Crown by the King of Italy and the attribution of powers to the Royal authority, reiterated the adoption of constitutional monarchy as system of government, illustrated the principles on which the judicial system was based, defined the rights and duties of citizens.

THE ALBANIAN UNITS OF THE ROYAL ITALIAN ARMY

With the merger of the armed forces of the two countries, the Albanian soldiers, including a good number of officers and non-commissioned officers, were admitted to serve not only in the Royal Italian Army but also in the Royal Italian Air Force and in the Royal Italian Navy[22]. On 24 May 1939 the Albanian Government entrusted the high command of the Gendarmerie to the Carabinieri General Crispino Agostinucci. The Albanian gendarmes were subsequently integrated into the *"Arma"* (Carabinieri are often referred to as the *"Arma"*, shortened name for Arma dei Carabinieri) organized from 17 October 1939 as follows: Carabinieri High Command of Albania (Tiranë, under the orders of General Agostinucci), Territorial Legion of Tiranë (groups from Tiranë, *Shkodër*, Durrës, Elbasan, Peshkopi, Kukës), Territorial Legion of Vlorë (groups of Vlorë, Berat, Gjirokastër, *Korça*)[23], for a total of 31 companies, 42 tenancies, and more than 200 stations. The ranks of the Carabinieri swelled further with the arrival of numerous soldiers from Italy. With the start of operations against Greece, a battalion of Italians and Albanians, made up of personnel from both Territorial Legions, and a platoon from the Tiranë Legion attached to the *"Siena"* Infantry Division, were added to the Carabinieri Sections assigned to the large units[24]. On 28 November 1940, a reorganization of the *"Arma"* was started. This measure led to the establishment of two Carabinieri Army Commands[25] (9th and 11th), three Carabinieri Battalions, of which one for the Higher Command of Armed Forces in Albania, one for the 9th Army and one for the 11th Army, one Carabinieri Squadron for the Higher Command of Armed Forces in Albania, two Carabinieri battalions for security needs and ten Territorial Carabinieri Battalions. The latter units were also employed in combat. The conclusion of the campaigns on the Balkan fronts reduced the effectives. At the end of 1942 the Carabinieri High Command of Albania included the Legions of Tiranë and Vlorë, five battalions (IV, VII, XIII, XVII and XXVII), Carabinieri of the IV and XXV Army Corps[26], Carabinieri of the Headquarters of the Higher Command of Armed Forces in Albania, Carabinieri of the Royal Air Force of Albania. At the beginning of the spring of 1943, the dismissal of all Albanian Carabinieri was ordered. This decision led to the inevitable dissolution of the Legions of Tiranë and Vlorë[27].

---

22 The Italian military academies trained most of the Albanian officers.
23 Many Albanians brought the *"alamari"*, the typical collar patches of the uniform worn by Carabinieri. The Albanian Carabiniere Gjanaj Rahman of the Tiranë Legion deserves to be mentioned, decorated with the Gold Medal for Military Valour in Memory, who fell in Lurth di Perlati on 21 November 1940 during an action carried out together with two younger comrades against a group of six dangerous outlaws.
24 On 28 October 1940, almost half of the officers and non-commissioned officers and approximately two thirds of the lance corporals and Carabinieri serving in the two Territorial Legions of the *"Arma"* were made up of soldiers of Albanian nationality. On 20 May 1940 the Italian XXVI Army Corps included 2,966 Albanian Carabinieri. On 20 February 1941, 2,409 Albanians of the *"Arma"* (58 officers) were operating in the territory. Under the date of April 12, the effectives rose to 2,478 (57 officers).
25 The 9th and 11th Armies were created on 9 November 1940 and subordinated to the newly established Higher Command of Armed Forces in Albania. The latter name was then assumed by the 9th Army on 1 July 1941.
26 It is worth remembering that starting from 22 October 1940 the XXVI Army Corps Command, a direct transformation of the Albanian Army Corps Command, stopped exercising the functions inherited from the High Command of Troops in Albania, dissolved on 1 December 1939. In fact, it took over a narrower physiognomy and handed over part of the divisions assigned to it to the newly established *"Ciamuria"* Army Corps, renamed XXV Army Corps on 9 November 1940.
27 At the same time as the dismissal of the Albanian soldiers, a reorganization hypothesis was put forward which would have redesigned the structure of the *"Arma"* in Albania, centered on a Carabinieri Command, three groups (of which only one already formed), nine battalions (five of which to be created ex novo), an independent company. However, this intention was only partially pursued, probably also hindered by the precipitation of events that led to the Armistice.

The Albanian Border Guard was instead subsumed into the Italian Guardia di Finanza[28]. On 30 April 1939, the Guardia di Finanza Command of Albania was established, at the head of which was placed Colonel Enrico Palandri. In the spring of 1940, a plan was drawn up for the use of the Guardia di Finanza units stationed in the "Land of Eagles". The border with Greece was split into two sectors (Gjirokastër and *Korça*) including sub-sectors (for which the companies were responsible) and surveillance sections (under the responsibility of the tenancies), with the presence of a battalion. The Yugoslav border was in turn split into three sectors (Kukës, Librazhd and *Shkodër*), which were also divided into subsectors and surveillance sections. The Albanian coast was split into four sectors (Durrës, Sarandë, *Shëngjin* and Vlorë), each divided into ten subsectors. In the summer of 1940 it was decided to form three battalions with personnel already available in Albania, personnel recalled from Italy and Albanian soldiers from the suppressed Border Guard. In view of the attack on Greece, some units were attached to the Italian divisions. The difficult situation that arose in November 1940 led to the formation of a new battalion (the I Battalion), and the sending of the III Battalion to the front. The needs linked to the surveillance of the wider Albanian borders resulting from the outcome of the operations against Greece and Yugoslavia imposed the creation of seven battalions (IV, V, VI, VII, VIII, IX and X). Of these, the IV, the IX and the X Battalions were placed under the control of the 2nd Italian Army in charge of the occupation of Slovenia and Dalmatia. Other battalions depended on the Higher Command of Armed Forces in Albania: the III Battalion (in Debar, Macedonia) and the VII Battalion (in Prizren, Kosovo) were assigned to the XIV Army Corps, the II Battalion (in Kotor, Montenegro) and the VI Battalion (in Cettigne, Montenegro) became part of the XVII Army Corps, the I Battalion was deployed on the island of Corfù (Greece). From the end of 1942 and until 8 September 1943, the Guardia di Finanza of Albania included the *Shkodër* Legion on three battalions (Dibër, Durrës, *Shkodër*) and a naval station (Durrës), the Tiranë Legion on four battalions (Gjirokastër, *Korça*, Tiranë, Vlorë) and a naval station (Vlorë), the III Battalion (in Tetovo, Macedonia), the VII Battalion (in Prizren) and the XV Battalion (in Peja, Kosovo). An Armed Police Corps also operated in Albania (directed by an Italian inspector in 1941) characterized by a large presence of Italian officers, non-commissioned officers and agents, established by Lieutenant's Decree of 31 August 1939. A reorganization mainly aimed at increasing the presence of Albanians in the Police started two and a half years later. Of the over 500 non-commissioned officers and agents serving in the Corps, many were of Albanian nationality. The units belonging to the arms, corps and specialties of the Royal Italian Army which were exclusively or largely made up of Albanian soldiers will be examined in greater detail below[29].

Albanian Infantry Battalions
Six of the seven Infantry battalions already in the army of King Zog were incorporated into the Royal Italian Army. On paper, the overall strength of each of these units was around 800 men, distributed in a Headquarters company, three rifle companies (each on a command platoon and three rifle platoons) and a machine gun company (on four platoons). The armament was essentially that used by the Italian infantry at the time although it did not normally include a sufficient supply of support weapons with the exception of a limited number of 45 mm Brixia Mod. 35 mortars and 8

---

28 In May 1940, the Guardia di Finanza units assigned to the Italian XXVI Army Corps included 955 Albanians (58 officers) in their ranks. On 20 February 1941 the number of those present in the area dropped to 697 (40 officers). On 12 April 1941 there were 693 Albanians with the *"Yellow Flames"* (the number of officers remained unchanged). *"Yellow Flames"* is the nickname for the Guardia di Finanza units (the collar patches applied to the jacket are stylized yellow flames).
29 On 20 May 1940, a total force of 6,459 soldiers of Albanian nationality was present in the mountain infantry divisions of the Royal Italian Army forming part of the XXVI Italian Army Corps. Albanian soldiers were distributed as follows: 1,995 men (62 officers) in the *"Venezia"* Division, 1,984 men (56 officers) in the *"Ferrara"* Division, 2,480 men (65 officers) in the *"Arezzo"* Division. At the same date there were 17 Albanians (12 officers) in the *"Julia"* Alpine Infantry Division and 5 Albanians (all officers) in the *"Centauro"* Armored Division.

mm Breda Mod. 37 machine guns. The Albanian *"Gramos"* and *"Dajti"* Battalions were assigned respectively to the 47th and 48th Regiments of the *"Ferrara"* Mountain Infantry Division and employed since the beginning of hostilities with Greece. The *"Ferrara"* Division had to take possession of the Kalibaki road junction and then march towards Gianina. The advance of the Italian infantry, supported by the *"Centauro"* Armored Division, was to develop along two lines. The *"Dajti"* Battalion was attached to the *"Colonna Trizio"*, which moved from the north, the *"Gramos"* Battalion was part of the *"Colonna Sapienza"*[30], which proceeded further south. Both units were involved in the first challenging battles. The 225th and 226th Regiments of the *"Arezzo"* Mountain Infantry Division respectively incorporated the Albanian Battalions *"Kaptina"* and *"Korata"*[31]. Stationed since May 1940 in the Shkodër area, with the start of operations against Greece the *"Arezzo"* Division moved to the vicinity of Peshkopi and at the end of October positioned itself south-east of Lake Ohrid. In many cases the Albanian units reached their destinations after exhausting foot marches. In a report dated 14 November 1940 signed by an Italian police advisor, sent to General Ubaldo Soddu, supreme commander of the troops in Albania, we read: *"On the morning of the 11th, a battalion of Albanian soldiers under the command of Major Fuad Dibra passed through Tirana, coming from Shkodër. They gave the impression of poor military spirit and deficient equipment. All the members of this unit including commander and officers with the exception of those two or three who attended military school in Italy have shown that they are disinterested in the war"*. The Albanian major cited in the text, at that time commander of the *"Korata"* Battalion, protested strongly against the lack of vehicles for long transfers. In hindsight, it was a problem that gripped many units of the Royal Italian Army during the Greek campaign. It is known that the conflict against Greece did not enjoy great popularity among the Albanian infantry. This moral fragility was often accompanied by insufficient preparation of the officers and incomplete training of the troops. Deficiencies of this kind affected to an even more dramatic extent the performance of the *"Tomori"* Battalion, attached to the 83rd Regiment of the *"Venezia"* Mountain Infantry Division[32]. In the imminence of the attack on Greece, the large unit was deployed between the locations of Trebishti and Bilishti, near Lakes Prespa and Ohrid. On 3 November 1940 the Italian Division was on the line. Moving from the Librazhd area, the *"Tomori"* Battalion also reached its destination, near Bitinckë, after a tiring march. The Albanian battalion, 834 men strong (12 officers), after reaching the vicinity of Mount Vipiakut, had to head towards Vërnik and conquer the Lapishtit - Strene ridge. The action, set for 6.45 am of 4 November 1940, progressed until it was supported by artillery and support weapons since soon the Albanian troops advancing in the open were targeted by enfilade fire from Greek machine guns. Without shelter, the bulk of the unit fell back in disorder and disbanded. Shortly before 2.00 pm, the Albanian Major Spiro Koxhobashi, commander of the *"Tomori"* Battalion, communicated to Colonel Ferdinando Graziani, commander of the 83rd Regiment, that together with a dozen officers and a hundred soldiers he still remained in the line. Considering the impossibility of maintaining the positions achieved, the remnants of the unit were recalled to the rear. The *"Tarabosh"* Battalion was included in the 84th Infantry Regiment of the *"Venezia"* Division. For some time this Albanian unit remained headquartered in Tirana together with the 3rd *"Granatieri di Sardegna"* Regiment which also took care of its training. Following the *"Tomori"* Battalion débacle and therefore in order to avoid the recurrence of phenomena that the Italian military authorities considered as worrying manifestations of disobedience by the Albanian military, the *"Tarabosh"* Battalion was also diverted from deployment in the line and assigned to execution of road works. Even if the Italian commands

---

30 Colonels Trizio and Sapienza were respectively in command of the 47th and 48th Regiments of the *"Ferrara"* Division.
31 Separated from the *"Arezzo"* Division, the *"Kaptina"* and *"Korata"* Battalions were subsequently assigned to support the *"Julia"* Division and from August 1940 reunited in a group under the command of Albanian Colonel Prenk Pervizi.
32 Until May 1940 the *"Tomori"* depended on the 84th Infantry Regiment based in Elbasan, being only under the administrative control of the 83rd Infantry Regiment.

in Albania ended up considering the infantry units made up of local elements unreliable, there was no lack of complaints from the Albanian side regarding the methods of employment of these formations, the main interpreter of which was probably Colonel Prenk Pervizi[33] who complained about an excessively unscrupulous use of the Albanian units attached to Italian divisions. The performance offered by the Albanian battalions employed in the line was the subject of a report drawn up by General Ubaldo Soddu, sent to the Deputy Chief of Staff, General Mario Roatta. The judgment of the superior commander of the troops in Albania appears severe but balanced: while taking into due consideration factors such as the poor quality of the majority of the officers and the inconsistency of morale, he does not neglect the difficult tactical situations in which the Albanian soldiers sometimes operated. Soddu underlined that since there was no shortage of soldiers who remained firmly in the line, there was the belief that the Italian Army could count on more effective elements at the end of a valid training program. A new larger unit called *"Scanderbeg"* Group was formed in Shijak with what was left of the 6 Infantry Battalions and the 4 75/13 Batteries[34]. A two-battalion training regiment made up of elements of the Group was entrusted with the defense of the Albanian coast near Shkodër shortly before the start of the conflict with Yugoslavia. Albanian infantry wore Italian uniforms. The use of the *plisa* or *qeleshe*, the classic Albanian white headdress, remained widespread. Furthermore, the use of the Italian M33 helmet in combat is documented. The jackets, at least in theory, were supposed to have the collar patches of the Italian regiments in which the Albanian battalions were incorporated. On 2 March 1940 the adoption of particular stars (*"stellette"*) for the collar patches carried by Albanian soldiers of the Royal Italian Army[35], distinguishable from the Italian ones as they were surmounted by the Scanderbeg helmet (as established for the Albanian Royal Guard) and made of white metal was prescribed . However, this provision did not have immediate application, so at the beginning of the operations against Greece the uniforms of the Albanian soldiers were still accompanied by the traditional Italian stars.

Albanian Regional Volunteer Battalions
At the beginning of the autumn of 1940, the General Lieutenancy of the King evaluated the opportunity of creating eight formations of volunteers from various regions of Albania who would be tasked with protecting and facilitating the Italian advance into Greek territory, making use of the proverbial skill of the Albanians in mountain fighting. At the head of each unit would have been placed an Albanian major or an authoritative exponent of the local community, in fact subordinate to an Italian officer (of equal or higher rank). The Albanian Regional Volunteer Battalions were supposed to consist of a command and three (or four) companies. In reality, given the limited time available for the recruitment and training of men, it was only possible to form six battalions compared to the eight initially planned[36]. Since no detailed directives had been issued regarding the

---
33 Albanian infantry colonel, admitted from 18 December 1939 to the roles of the Royal Italian Army, in 1940 Prenk Pervizi was assigned to the Italian command of the Korça sector. He attended the Military Academy of Vienna (1914-1918) and the War School of Turin (1930 -1933) with profit. In the two-year period 1935 – 36 he was part of the International Commission of Foreign Observers in the Ethiopian War. On 16 January 1941 he was appointed Knight of the Order of SS. Maurice and Lazarus. In 1942 he was promoted to brigadier general and in October 1943, with the rank of lieutenant general, he became Minister of Defence in the government of the new Albanian State.
34 More precisely, under the date of 24 November 1940 the Albanian Higher Troop Command ordered the creation of the *"Scanderbeg"* Albanian Battalions Group, under the orders of Alfredo D'Andrea, former commander of the Albanian Royal Guard stationed in Rome. The first units transferred to the Group were the *"Tomori"*, *"Gramos"* and *"Kaptina"* Battalions.
35 The stars with Scanderbeg's helmet also adorned the uniforms of the Albanians serving in the Royal Italian Air Force and in the Royal Italian Navy. In the first case the Albanian stars, in white metal, were applied on the lapel, in the second case, made of white thread, they were worn on the sailor's collar. The adoption of badges and decorations characteristic of the Italian armed forces was also envisaged.
36 About 1,000 men were drafted. Given the insufficient availability of personnel, the units formed with volunteers could not be considered real battalions, being such in name but not in fact.

uniform to be adopted, the volunteers would have had to wear the typical costume of the region of origin and carry on their right arm a band with the colors of the Albanian flag (red and black) decorated centrally with a star of metal placed on an Italian tricolour cockade. Another wide red and black band would have encircled the waist while the rank insignia of the Royal Italian Army would have been affixed to the left of the chest. However, it is possible that some formations made use of more appropriate items of military clothing of Italian manufacture, the distribution of which had been planned. On 28 October 1940 the 1st and 2nd Battalions, formed by Albanian volunteers of Chamuriot origin[37], were placed at the western end of the Italian deployment, to be used in support of the "*Raggruppamento del Litorale*", a combat group led by General Carlo Rivolta, including the 3rd "*Granatieri di Sardegna*" Regiment, the 7th Cavalry Regiment "*Lancieri di Milano*" and the 6th Cavalry Regiment "*Lancieri di Aosta*", and in favour of the "*Siena*" Infantry Division, a unit included in the XXV Army Corps. The forces moving along the coastal strip had been assigned the objective of creating a bridgehead on the Kalamas River, an essential condition for proceeding with the conquest of Preveza, Louros and Arta. The I Volunteer Battalion, at the orders of Major Aziz Çami assisted by the Italian Major Francesco Pescosolido, was initially placed in support of Italian Cavalry units. The II Volunteer Battalion, commanded by Major Skënder Çami, was instead immediately attached to the 3rd "*Granatieri*" Regiment, in compliance with the orders given by Major Ugo Chiaravalli, Senior Officer at the disposal of the regimental command. The commander of the II Battalion revealed in a written report that, after having overcome the first line of Greek resistance, his soldiers passed through various villages of Ciamuria. In those places, inhabited largely by Albanians, the population provided additional volunteers to the formation which thus saw its size increase. Placed in the front line and 300 men strong, the Battalion achieved other successes against the enemy and was among the first units to cross the Kalamas. Coinciding with the start of the Greek counteroffensive, the 1st and 2nd Battalions were reunited into a single larger group[38], but in a short time the men, almost devoid of food and ammunition, were taken to the rear and placed on leave. The III Battalion (formed in Gjirokastër) was attached to the "*Siena*" Infantry Division with its 90 men and placed under the command of Captain Buonaccorsi. The IV Albanian Volunteer Battalion (established in Permeti) was attached to the "*Ferrara*" Division. Until mid-November 1940, when it was possible to at least partially increase the number of effectives, the consistent strength of the IV Battalion[39] was equivalent to that of a company. The V Volunteer Battalion (created in Leskovik) was assigned to the "*Julia*" Alpine Division. The unit dissolved during the strenuous defense of the Konitza valley which had been occupied to facilitate the progression of the Alpine troops towards Metsovo. On 4 November 1940, the VI Battalion commanded by Major Vehip Runa, made up of around a hundred fighters originating from Kurvelesh (an area of southern Albania), concentrated in Ersekë from which it moved to conquer some Greek localities on the slopes of the Gramos Massif, among which Plikati and Denisko[40]. However, even this last formation could not avoid the same fate that befell

---

[37] The opportunity to use Albanian units alongside Italian ones in the Greek campaign also derived from propaganda intentions. The creation of a "Greater Albania" achievable through the annexation of territories situated within the Greek and Yugoslav borders inhabited largely by ethnic Albanian populations was in fact a clear objective of Italy. The Albanian and Italian press had long been committed to resolutely supporting the Albanian irredentist movement of Chamuria, an area between the southern border of Albania, the Ionian coast up to the city of Prevesa and the Gianina region. It was Galeazzo Ciano in particular who assumed the role of tutelary deity of Albania. In some Roman circles it was ironically whispered that the Italian Minister of Foreign Affairs intended to transform the "Land of Eagles" into a re-edition of the Grand Duchy of Tuscany or into his personal fiefdom. However, Chamuria was not annexed to Albania after the capitulation of Greece.
[38] On 11 November 1940 the formation commanded by Skënder Çami passed to the Italian XXV Army Corps.
[39] Cavalry Major Mario Grandi (decorated with Bronze Medal for Military Valour) led the IV Albanian Volunteer Battalion in various successful actions.
[40] The inadequacy of clothing and insufficient personnel were some of the factors that penalized the volunteer units employed at the front. The extent of these difficulties can be effectively deduced from the final considerations contained in a report dated 16 November 1940 by the Albanian Major Runa, sent to the commander of the "*Bari*" Infantry Division. We

the others: they all disbanded or were withdrawn from the front before the arrival of Winter. A few dozen Albanians from Chamuria not enlisted in Volunteer Battalions were employed as guides and also used to carry out sabotage tasks.

Albanian Anti-Aircraft Machine Gun Battalions
A circular dated 31 May 1940 sanctioned the establishment in Tiranë and Berat of two Albanian Anti-Aircraft Machine Gun Battalions (I and II), each structured around Headquarters, four (or five) companies and four (or five) spotting platoons. The soldiers of these units almost certainly wore the classic Italian uniform completed by the red and white collar patches of the machine gun battalions, on which the Albanian stars should have been affixed.

Albanian artillery batteries
In 1940 the Royal Italian Army included four 75/13 batteries (4 pack howitzers each), served by Albanian personnel. One of these, the *"Drin"* Battery[41], was incorporated into the 14th Artillery Regiment of the *"Ferrara"* Division at the outbreak of hostilities with Greece. A support battery of 75/13 pack howitzers under the orders of the Albanian lieutenant Lama was part of the 6th Cavalry Regiment *"Lancieri di Aosta"*, employed on the Greek-Albanian front. On 20 May 1940, 638 Albanian soldiers were in service with the artillery of the XXVI Italian Army Corps, 30 of whom were officers. On 26 April 1942 the 275th 75/27 *"Semani"* Battery of the Border Guard, made up of personnel from the dissolved 75/13 battery of the same name, was formed. The men of this unit wore Italian uniforms probably bearing on the collar the single-pointed green patch with yellow threads characteristic of the artillery of the Border Guard, with Albanian stars. On 20 June 1943 this Albanian battery appears assigned to the *"Shkodër* Subsector" (*Border Guard Sector "Z" Shkodër - Kosovo* with Headquarters in Prizren).

Albanian Squadron Group of the 7th Cavalry Regiment *"Lancieri di Milano"*
The 7th Cavalry Regiment *"Lancieri di Milano"*, deployed in Albania in June 1940, incorporated an Albanian Squadron Group[42].

Albanian engineers
Even though the formation of two engineer companies with Albanian personnel was planned[43], there is no certainty about the actual existence of these units. However, it is well established that on 20 May 1940, 250 Albanian engineers (7 officers) were present in the Italian XXVI Army Corps.

Albanian personnel of the Services of the Italian XXVI Army Corps
On 20 May 1940, 1,183 (99 officers) Albanians were part of the services of the Italian XXVI Army Corps. An Albanian pack train unit included in the *"Raggruppamento del Litorale"* was employed to transport food and various supplies.

---

read verbatim: *"Your Excellency, the sixth battalion made up of the Kurveleshas is composed of around a hundred people. A force of one hundred people cannot face even a guard post and even more so cannot sustain an offensive and face an enemy with modernized forces and in much greater numbers. Therefore I ask you if it is possible to order where it is necessary that my battalion is increased by 400-500 Albanian people, from the regions of Kurveleshi or Skrapar and be equipped with all the necessary means that today's war requires, as well as provided with food and clothing. Because in the current conditions I wouldn't be able to make my contribution at all"*.
41 The other Albanian 75/13 batteries were called *"Mathi"*, *"Vjosë"* and *"Semani"*. On 1 November 1939 they were assigned respectively to the 3rd Mountain Artillery Regiment, the 30th Artillery Regiment and the 19th Artillery Regiment.
42 Originally formed as an Albanian Cavalry platoon of the *"Aosta"* Squadron Group.
43 See Marenglem Kasmi, "Lufta italo-greke 1940-1941 dhe të rënët grekë në Shqipëri", https://alb-spirit.com/2017/01/13/lufta-italo-greke-1940-1941-dhe-te -renet-greke-ne-shqiperi/.

"Bottai's Irregulars"

On 2 April 1941 the Duce appointed Giuseppe Bottai Inspector General of the irregular forces of Albania. The Minister of National Education would have had the task of organizing various Albanian armed bands in the border areas with Yugoslavia. The creation of the first militias can be traced back to November 1940. The name *"Bottai's Irregulars"* refers to these units as a whole, made up of ethnic Albanian civilians coming from local districts or originating from Kosovo, Macedonia, Montenegro, under the command of political exponents, notables or military officers[44]. In the spring of 1941, the *"ringleader"* Giuseppe Bottai had around 3,500 men at his orders. These irregular troops, divided into rather heterogeneous groups, were mostly armed with Model 91 rifles and dressed in typical regional costumes. Some of the most relevant formations were the group of Mirdita strong with 1,000 fighters, the three groups that operated in the Dibër District, for a total of 1,080 militiamen and the group of Shkodër with 400 men. In the framework of the upcoming operations against Yugoslavia, the irregulars led by Bottai were given a dual task: to hinder any advances of Yugoslav Royal Army into Albanian territory and to support Italian counter-offensives. On 6 April 1941 and in the immediately following days, Yugoslav forces attacked in the direction of Shkodër and in other sectors, causing an initial retreat of the Italian lines. The reaction of the Albanian militias was not long in coming. One of the bloodiest clashes occurred in the mountainous region of Dukagjini, where 400 volunteers led by the deputy secretary of the Albanian Fascist Party Kol Bib Mirakaj[45] inflicted heavy losses on the enemy. The Italian military leaders in Albania judged with satisfaction the performance of the Albanian irregular formations, consisting of guerrillas animated by a strong feeling of revenge towards the Serbs. With the Axis victory over Yugoslavia, large areas of Kosovo and some areas of western Macedonia and southern Montenegro were annexed to Albania. In these lands Italy implemented a policy in favor of the ethnic Albanian populations. Tiranë authorities were given the task of choosing the prefects, quaestors and secretaries of the Federations of the Albanian Fascist Party in the new regions of "Greater Albania". Ethnic Albanian notables and personalities were entrusted with the administration and defense of cities and villages. Especially in Kosovo, new militias known as *"vulnetari"* (volunteers), were formed to protect local communities. These Albanian bands were used to fight the partisans, first alongside the Italian troops and after 8 September 1943 together with the Germans.

Albanian Rifle Regiments

Once the two major campaigns in the Balkans were concluded, drawing on the personnel of the pre-existing battalions and proceeding with new recruitments, three *"Albanian Rifles"* Regiments (*"Cacciatori d'Albania"*) were created. These Albanian infantry units of the Royal Italian Army were primarily used in anti-partisan repression and territorial surveillance[46]. Each regiment was made up of Headquarters (including the commander and eight officers in addition to the Headquarters Company divided into two platoons), two Rifle battalions (each with a Headquarters Company and three rifle companies), a machine gun company (with Headquarters Platoon and three machine gun platoons with twelve weapons), a support 65/17 battery (4 pieces) and should have included a total

---

44 Among the militiamen coordinated by Bottai there were also former guerrillas of the Kosovar separatist formations of the *Kaçak* who had already been supported by Italy in the years between the two World Wars. In the summer of 1941 sub-units of the *"Puglie"* Division, to which the Albanian *"Gramos"* and *"Korata"* Battalions (used to quell a revolt in Montenegro) had already been added, were reinforced with 26 bands of Kosovar guerrillas for a total of 1,600 men. In April 1942 the number of effectives rose to 3,000. These irregulars were supposed to help repel any incursions by the Serbs into Kosovar territory.
45 Decorated with a Silver Medal for Military Valour for having opposed the enemy forces at the head of his volunteers despite the wounds sustained during the battle.
46 A circular dated 14 March 1942 gave the units the name of 1st, 2nd and 3rd *"Albanian Rifles"* Regiments.

of 1,705 men in its ranks, of which 66 officers and 1,639 non-commissioned officers and troops[47]. With the exception of the commanding colonel, some officers and a small number of specialists who were Italian, all the other soldiers were Albanian. The equipment of each regiment also included 9 officer's horses, 304 packhorses, 60 draft horses, 30 carts, 22 bicycles, 3 motorcycles, 1 car or light truck. In the spring of 1943, a fourth regiment was established, enlisting young Kosovar recruits. Together with the 1st Regiment[48], the 4th Regiment should have formed the 1st *"Albanian Rifle Brigade"*, a unit that should have been placed at the orders of Prenk Pervizi, who rose to the rank of general. In the late summer of 1943, the 1st Regiment was an integral part of the *"Puglie"* Infantry Division, stationed in Kosovo, under which the 4th Regiment was also placed. The 2nd Regiment[49] had instead been attached to the *"Parma"* Infantry Division which garrisoned an area between Tepeleni, Gjirokastër, Himara and Vlorë with counter-guerrilla duties. In Peja, at 6.00 am on 9 September 1943 (the day following the announcement of the Armistice), the commander of the 1st *"Albanian Rifles"* Regiment took note that the unit under his command was surrounded by German troops who demanded the surrender of their weapons. A short time later, the commander of the 4th Regiment also announced that an Albanian officer had taken command of the unit to join the German forces, leaving the Italian soldiers free. In the same hectic days the 2nd and 3rd Regiments[50], decimated by defections, were disbanded. The *"Albanian Rifles"* wore Italian uniforms. Red pentagonal insignia crossed by a black transverse band, threaded with Savoy blue and adorned with Albanian stars were affixed to the collar of the jacket as prescribed by a circular dated 29 March 1942.

Albanian Royal Guard
The *"Albanian Royal Guard"* was responsible for the Guard of Honor Service to Victor Emmanuel III, King of Italy and Albania, Emperor of Ethiopia, and for the surveillance of the Quirinale Palace. It was formed immediately after the conclusion of Operation Oltre Mare Tirana, organized into 5 companies and then quickly transferred to Rome, where it remained until the Armistice[51]. On 29 April 1939 the Guards swore loyalty to the sovereign. On 28 November 1939, the twenty-seventh anniversary of the independence of the "Land of Eagles" from the Ottoman Empire, the *"Albanian Royal Guard"* Battalion received the war flag in the courtyard of the *"Prince of Naples"* barracks in Rome[52]. During the Guard of Honor services, the soldiers wore a characteristic dress uniform available in two versions based on the traditional costumes of northern and southern Albania[53]. For the Northern uniform, tight-fitting white fustian trousers (*çedike*) were designed, the flared bottom of which was characterized by false red gaiters surrounded by embroidered threads.

---

47 The armament of the *"Albanian Rifles"* Regiments was similar to that of the other infantry regiments of the Royal Italian Army and included various models of the Carcano 91/38 rifle and Breda model 30 and 37 machine guns. The shortage of 65/17 pieces meant that in many cases these were replaced with 75/13 mountain howitzers.
48 Formed on 1 October 1942, it included the *"Gramos"* and *"Korata"* Battalions and the *"Vjosë"* Battery.
49 Made up of the *"Tarabosh"* and *"Dajti"* Battalions and the *"Mathi"* Battery.
50 It included the *"Tomori"* and *"Kaptina"* Battalions as well as the *"Drin"* Battery.
51 For a short period the Battalion moved away from Rome. At the outbreak of the war it joined the *"Granatieri di Sardegna"* Division, of which it was an integral part, moving to the Western Front but without taking part in any combat. In November 1941 the Battalion was reorganized into 3 companies.
52 The Guard was part of the 1st Granatieri (Grenadier) Regiment, belonging to the 21st Infantry Division *"Granatieri di Sardegna"*. Until 1 April 1940 the Albanian Guards were under the orders of the Italian lieutenant colonel Alfredo D'Andrea. Subsequently, the equal rank Pasquale Lissoni was appointed commander of the Battalion. The unit also included a Military Fanfare. The creation of a second battalion (a unit to also be used in combat) out of three companies based in Tiranë was planned.
53 In fact, the diversity of costumes also reflected the division of the Albanian language into two main dialects, the Gheg of the North and the Tosk of the South. The differences between the two dialects are fundamentally phonetic and not lexical. The geographical demarcation line between the Gheg and the Tosk can be roughly coincided with the course of the Shkumbini River. The motto of the Albanian Guards part of the Royal Italian Army, borrowed from the time of King Zog, was *"Gati me vdekë për Mbret!"*, that is *"Ready to die for the King!"*.

These, which were gold for officers and black for non-commissioned officers and troops, formed a frog that extended over the lower surface of the leg. Other more showy frogs embroidered with the same colors adorned the upper part of the thighs. The Southern uniform was instead characterized by a white kilt, called *"fustanella"*, similar to that of the Greek euzones although longer, worn over the trousers and by white felt greaves stopped at the knee, also ending in false red gaiters threaded in the same way as those that adorned the typical trousers of the Northern outfit. The other items of clothing were essentially common to both uniform models. The shirt, white with Albanian stars on the collar, sported red handguards edged in gold for officers and black for non-commissioned officers and troops. The embroidery that embellished the red waistcoat edged in black, worn on the shirt, was made in the same shades (gold for officers, black for non-commissioned officers and troops). A woolen sash in the Albanian national colors (red and black) was around the waist. Above this band the officers wore a strap of the same colors on the buckle of which was a double-headed eagle surmounted by Scanderbeg's helmet. The non-commissioned officers and the troops were instead provided with a twelve-pocket leather cartridge belt on which the bayonet scabbard was also placed. The ranks were affixed to the shirt: the officers, whose outfit was enriched by a blue scarf, wore them on their handguards, the non-commissioned officers and the troops on the sleeves. The white Albanian headdress (*qeleshe*), without decorations, was another element common to both versions of the uniforms, as were the gloves, which were also white. The members of the military band were dressed in the uniform of the North. The Albanian Guards also wore the other uniforms provided for the Infantry of the Royal Italian Army. The ordinary uniform (marching and combat uniform) was therefore the one normally used by Italian infantrymen. The rank insignia were also the same. The epaulettes bore a double-headed eagle in golden tinsel and a button depicting Scanderbeg's unmistakable helmet, also reproduced on the buttons of the jacket. On the lapel (often in black velvet for officers) were applied deep red, practically purple, frogs on a black background, adorned with Albanian stars. On the helmets there was an exclusive mask frieze of the Albanian Guards, black in color and 92 mm high, reproducing Scanderbeg's helmet coupled with the VE monogram of King Victor Emmanuel III. The Great Uniform obviously had differences compared to the ordinary one. A blue scarf, a red and black strap of the same type provided for the dress uniform and a ceremonial saber distinguished the officers' uniform. Both the officers and the graduates and the troops also carried aiguillettes attached to both epaulettes and wore white gloves.

▲ Italian Grenadiers of the 3rd Regiment affix the stars on the collar of the uniforms worn by the Albanian soldiers of the *"Tarabosh"* Battalion.

▼ The infantrymen of the *"Tarabosh"* Battalion receive the Italian stars. The Albanian ones, surmounted by Scanderbeg's helmet and made of white metal, will be introduced later.

▲ The commander of the *"Tarabosh"* Battalion is about to swear (Tirana, 30 July 1939). Before being integrated into the 84th Infantry Regiment of the *"Venezia"* Division, the *"Tarabosh"* Battalion was headquartered in Tirana with the 3rd *"Granatieri di Sardegna"* Regiment.

▼ Mussolini reviews the infantrymen of an Albanian battalion.

▲ Benito Mussolini among the Albanian infantrymen (Berat, March 1941).

▼ The Albanian infantrymen standing at attention before the Duce. The uniforms are Italian ones, the headgear is the typical Albanian *qeleshe*. (Berat, 5 March 1941).

▲ A carabiniere of Albanian nationality portrayed with his decoration.

▲ This picture shows fighters belonging to Albanian armed bands organized by Giuseppe Bottai, deployed in the border areas with Yugoslavia (Spring 1941).

▼ Dressed in typical regional costumes, the *"Bottai's Irregulars"* wore an armband distinguished by the Albanian and Italian national colors.

▲ An "*Albanian Rifle*" Regiment receives the war flag.

▼ Group photo portraying some officers of an "*Albanian Rifle*" Regiment. The typical pentagonal patches in the colors of Albania and the House of Savoy are clearly distinguishable on the collars of the jackets.

▲ The *"Royal Albanian Guard"* is deployed to render the honours. Two flags are visible: that of the Shqiptar unit and that of the 1st Grenadier Regiment. Rome, 29 April 1939.

▼ Royal Albanian Guards in full dress uniform of the North are reviewed. Rome, 29 April 1939.

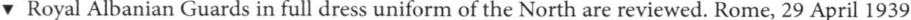

▲ Ceremony of handing over the flag to the *"Royal Albanian Guard"*. The *Guard*, which should have been formed into a Regiment, was officially contracted into a Battalion on 6 February 1940 due to the impossibility of filling the ranks.

▼ Another picture of the ceremony of handing over the flag to the *"Royal Albanian Guard"*. A different formula than usual was adopted for the ceremonial since the majority of the soldiers were of Muslim faith.

▲ The ceremony of handing over the flag to the *"Royal Albanian Guard"* took place in the courtyard of the *"Prince of Naples"* barracks in Rome.

▼ The *"Royal Albanian Guard"* received the flag on 28 November 1939, the date on which the twenty-seventh anniversary of the independence of the "Land of Eagles" from the Ottoman Empire occurred.

▲ The *"Royal Albanian Guard"* attends a ceremony in which the Duce intervenes.

▼ Guards in Southern uniform swear by raising their right arm. The troops collectively took the oath in the presence of General Pariani shouting *"Betoj!"* which in Albanian means *"I swear!"*. The officers swore individually in the hands of the commander of the 2nd Grenadier Regiment. Rome, 29 April 1939. At that time the unit consisted of about 600 men.

▲ Royal Albanian Guards in Southern uniform.
▼ Beautiful picture of Albanian Guards taking an oath.

▲ This photograph highlights further details of the two different dress uniforms envisaged for the *"Royal Albanian Guard"*.

▼ General Pariani talks with the commander of the *"Royal Albanian Guard"*.

▲ The Oath of the Albanian officer cadets. In the foreground, the Royal Guards in Great Uniform. In the background the *"Samoggia"* Barracks of the 2nd Grenadier Regiment. Rome, May 21, 1939.

▼ Albanian lieutenant Valentin Pervizi (first from left) aboard a Semovente M42 75/18. Son of General Prenk Pervizi, Valentin was commander of a self-propelled platoon of the *"Lancieri di Vittorio Emanuele II"* Regiment, part of the reconstituted *"Ariete"* Armored Division, a unit that opposed the German troops in the battle for the defense of Rome (8-10 September 1943). The inclusion of Albanian officers in the regiments stationed in Italy was authorized by Mussolini on 12 November 1939.

THE ALBANIAN FASCIST MILITIA

The *"Albanian Fascist Militia"* (Milizia Fascista Albanese, M.F.A.) was established by lieutenant decree of 18 September 1939. Part of the *"Voluntary Militia for National Security"* (the Italian Milizia Volontaria per la Sicurezza Nazionale, M.V.S.N.), and therefore under the orders of the Duce, the Albanian Militia was responsible for protection of public order and State security. Like the M.V.S.N., the M.F.A. was also divided into Legions (Regiments), Cohorts (Battalions), Centurias (Companies), Manipulos (Platoons) and Squads[54]. Each mobilized battalion included three (subsequently up to four) rifle companies, supported by platoons detached from the machine gun company employed by the Legion. Initially, thanks to the influx of the first volunteers (mostly Albanian citizens but also Italians resident in Albania), an Ordinary Legion and an Alpine Legion were established, both organized into three Cohorts. In June 1940 Francesco Jacomoni di San Savino, Lieutenant General of the King, reported in a writing how the Albanian Blackshirts were eager to fight for the construction of a "Greater Albania". In view of the hostilities against Greece, the 1st Blackshirt Assault Legion of the *"Albanian Fascist Militia"* was mobilized, organized into two training battalions (just over 1,000 men) under the command of Consul Giuseppe Volante[55]. The unit was assigned to the *"Ferrara"* Mountain Infantry Division. Elements of the II Battalion, which was part of the *"Solinas Column"*[56] of the *"Centauro"* Armored Division, had to start operations on the Greek-Albanian front. Around 5.30 am on 28 October 1940, a platoon of the 4th Company attacked the Perati bridge over the Sarandaporos River, a tributary of the Vjosë River, defeating the Greek soldiers who were guarding the border post after a brief firefight. In the immediately following days the Battalion continued to play the role of advanced element of the Italian column[57] tasked with attacking the strategic position of Kalibaki from the north. On 2 November his Blackshirts took the village of Mesovouni, located less than 10 km from the designated objective. The 1st Battalion instead began operations while remaining attached to the *"Ferrara"* Division as an element of the *"Colonna Sapienza"* which, launched along the Kakavia-Delvinaki-Krioneri-Sitaria route, was to invest Kalibaki from the south. At the end of November both battalions were withdrawn from the front line. With the opening of the Yugoslav front, the Legion was destined to reinforce the Italian XVII Armored Corps of General Giuseppe Pafundi. Already at the end of March 1941, the two battalions of Blackshirts were positioned not far from Borizanë, north of Tiranë, about to be transferred near *Shkodër*. In the days from 11 to 13 April the Albanian soldiers contributed to neutralizing the Yugoslav attacks in the Tarabosh-Kiri-Drin sector together with units of the *"Centauro"* Armored Division and elements of the *"Messina"* Infantry Division. After the defeat of Yugoslavia, the 1st Assault Legion was disbanded. The main task of the units formed starting from 1942 was the control of the territory[58]. The definitive organization of the *"Albanian Fascist Militia"*, foreseen since the autumn of 1939,

---
[54] In case of difference, the correspondence of the militia units with those of the army is indicated in brackets.
[55] In 1942 Giuseppe Volante was promoted to Consul General, thus becoming commander of the *"Albanian Fascist Militia"*, succeeding Gino Ballabio and Alessandro Biscaccianti. After the Armistice he joined the Italian Social Republic. He was head of the Inspectorate of the *"National Republican Railway Guard"* (*"Guardia Nazionale Repubblicana Ferroviaria"*) and commanded the 1st Anti-parachute and Anti-aircraft Division *"Etna"* of the National Republican Guard (*"Guardia Nazionale Repubblicana"*, G.N.R.).
[56] The column took its name from Colonel Gioacchino Solinas, commander of the 5th Bersaglieri Regiment.
[57] On 30 October the advanced units of the *"Solinas Column"* joined the *"Trizio Column"*, passing under the control of the *"Ferrara"* Division.
[58] In 1942 the *"Albanian Fascist Militia"* could be further expanded with personnel from the regions annexed to the "Land of Eagles". Ethnic Albanian Kosovars formed the VII Battalion of the 4th Legion (stationed in Prizren), a unit that fought with particular fury against local partisans. From October 1941 to March 1942, a centuria of the 4th Legion was called into service, also known as Special Company *"D"* (from Dukagjini, the recruitment area located near Shkodër) which was used for the surveillance of public order.

contemplated the following configuration[59], including the battalions mobilized during its existence:

M.F.A. Legions Group Command (Tiranë)

1st M.F.A. Legion (Tiranë)
- Permanent Cohorts: Tiranë, Durrës, Peshkopi
  - Mobilized Battalions: I, V, VI, X, XII

2nd M.F.A. Legion (Korça)
- Permanent Cohorts: Korça, Elbasan
  - Mobilized Battalions: XI

3rd M.F.A. Legion (Vlorë)
- Permanent Cohorts: Vlorë, Berat, Gjirokastër
  - Mobilized Battalions: III, VIII, XII, XIV

4th M.F.A. Legion (Shkodër)
- Permanent Cohorts: Shkodër, Kukës
  - Mobilized Battalions: II, IV, VII, IX

In addition to the ordinary *"Albanian Fascist Militia"*, two special militias were created with police functions, the *"Albanian Forest Militia"* (*"Milizia Forestale Albanese"*) and the *"Albanian Road Militia"* (*"Milizia Albanese della Strada"*), both dependent on the *"Voluntary Militia for National Security"*. The implementation of laws and provisions relating to forestry, the management of the woods and the direction of reforestation and mountain reclamation works, the creation and cultivation of nurseries and experimental fields were among the tasks entrusted to the *"Albanian Forest Militia"*[60]. The *"Albanian Road Militia"*[61] was responsible for the control of road traffic, the information service relating to road safety, the supervision of the conservation of road signs, and vehicle rescue operations. The *"Albanian Fascist Militia"* adopted the same uniform as the *"Voluntary Militia for National Security"*, essentially that of the Royal Italian Army with the exception of the shirt and tie which were black. The rank insignia were also those of the Italian militia as were the patches applied to the collar of the grey-green cloth jacket, which consisted of the traditional two-pointed black flames bearing metal little fasces. A circular humeral badge made of bakelite, red in color and edged in gold with the black double-headed eagle of Albania was worn on the left sleeve. Instead of the characteristic black fez, the Albanian Blackshirts wore a white felt headdress inspired by the local *qeleshe*, decorated on the front with the M.V.S.N. frieze, a fasce between two branches surmounted by a five-pointed star. The use of the puttees and the adoption of the M33 helmet in combat are documented. The men of the *"Albanian Forest Militia"* wore an Alpine hat without a feather (also used by the Alpine cohorts of the M.V.S.N.) and also made use of leather greaves. The armament of the M.F.A. was similar to that of the M.V.S.N.; obviously the typical dagger in the various models envisaged for officers, non-commissioned officers and troops was essential. In a document dated 26 November 1942 we read that the members of the Albanian militia had been awarded various rewards

---

59 In some photographs taken in the late summer of 1940, two labarums stand out which bear the following double inscriptions in Albanian and Italian: "LEGJONI I 11 <TIRANË> – 11ª LEGIONE <TIRANA>" and "LEGJONI I 13 <VLORË> – 13ª LEGIONE <VALONA >". These two Assault Legions were formed with 4 battalions drawn from each of the existing legions. The 1st Blackshirt Assault Legion of the *"Albanian Fascist Militia"* was created with elements from these units.
60 The *"Albanian Forest Militia"* was organized around a Legion Command, 3 Cohorts, 8 detached Commands and 60 minor Commands. The personnel were predominantly Albanian. Similarly to the 9 Legions present in Italy and the 2 Legions stationed in the Colonies and in the Empire, the unit was part of the *"National Forest Militia"* (*"Milizia Forestale Nazionale"*). Its exact denomination was 12th Legion *"National Forest Militia"*.
61 The *"Albanian Road Militia"* was organized around a Command Group of Departments and 7 Commands located in the main Albanian cities. The personnel were mainly of Italian nationality.

for military valour including 1 gold medal, 4 silver medals, 16 bronze medals and 77 war crosses. After the fall of the government presided over by the Duce, the *"Albanian Fascist Militia"* took the name of *"Albanian Volunteer Militia"* (*Milizia Volontaria Albanese*, M.V.A.). With the Armistice these formations dissolved and part of the soldiers probably ended up siding with the Germans or the partisans.

▲ An Albanian Blackshirt in the typical grey-green uniform and with the traditional white *qeleshe* worn on his head. On the left sleeve the red humeral circular badge edged in gold bearing the black double-headed eagle of Albania is clearly visible. Two-pointed black flames embellished by metal fasces were applied to the collar of the jacket.

▲ Soldiers from one of the three Cohorts of the Alpine Legion of the *"Albanian Fascist Militia"*.

▲ A unit of *"Albanian Fascist Militia"* awaits review.

▼ Deployment of Albanian Blackshirts reviewed by the military authorities.

▲ Albanian Blackshirts parade at the Roman pass. Article 1 of the lieutenant decree of 18 September 1939 n. 91 specified that the Duce was General Commander of the *"Albanian Fascist Militia"*.

▼ Albanian Blackshirts march armed with Carcano muskets mod. 91/38.

▲ Another image of an *"Albanian Fascist Militia"* parade.

▼ Two Albanian Blackshirts train with a Fiat Revelli Mod. 1935 machine gun.

▲ A centurion of the *"Albanian Fascist Militia"* receives a decoration from King Victor Emmanuel III. In this picture you can also recognize Ugo Cavallero, Chief of the General Staff. *Shkodër*, 15 May 1941.

◄ The Italian weekly newspaper *Domenica del Corriere* of 8 December 1940 celebrates the glorious death of an Albanian Blackshirt, decorated with the Gold Medal for Military Valour in memory.

RECONSTITUTION AND EMPLOYMENT OF THE ALBANIAN ARMY AFTER THE ARMISTICE

The Armistice of 8 September 1943 also marked the fate of Albania (linked to that of Italy from 16 April 1939), since from that date the Germans took control of the entire country. The occupiers entrusted administrative powers to a renewed nationalist and pro-German executive supported by the High Council of Regency[62], a collegiate body designed to temporarily represent the leadership of the new State. From a formal point of view, Albania became an independent and neutral country: the government undertook to ensure control of the territory, obtaining in exchange from Germany the guarantee of being able to maintain sovereignty over the regions annexed after the victorious campaigns of the Axis in the Balkans. The revival of autonomous Albanian regular armed forces under German supervision encountered multiple difficulties, also due to the shortage of instructors in the local ranks. The reorganization of the army was entrusted to Prenk Pervizi, who assumed the position of Minister of Defence with the rank of general. The project, illustrated in a typescript dated December 1943 and remained largely unimplemented, essentially concerned the structure and methods of employment of the Infantry, the Gendarmerie, the Border Guard and the volunteer troops. At that time, the recruitment of new personnel, sufficient to form at least four new infantry battalions, should have taken place only in the recently annexed territories. As we have seen, two Albanian infantry units of the Royal Italian Army were operational in Kosovo, namely the 1st and 4th *"Albanian Rifle"* Regiments which on 9 September had gone over to the Germans. According to Pervizi[63] it would have been necessary to establish two more infantry regiments in Dibër and *Shkodër*, both divided into three battalions and including artillery units, enlisting men (75% reservists) from the regions already inside the old national borders. In reality it was possible to count on a more modest force than hoped for, equal to around 4,800 soldiers. However, formations of Kosovar volunteers led by local leaders flowed into the two formations inherited from the Italian army. These formations certainly contributed to reinforce Albanian infantry, used against the partisans until the end of hostilities[64]. The units were equipped with the weapons that had been distributed to the *"Albanian Rifle"* Regiments, materials which were also available in fair quantities in the abandoned depots of the Royal Italian Army. The Gendarmerie, an integral part of the Shqiptar armed forces, was reconstituted in March 1943, when it was spun off from the Carabinieri[65]. With Royal Decree n. 387 of 29 March 1943, all the Carabinieri of Albanian nationality were dismissed to be included in the Gendarmerie which assumed the role played up to that point by the *"Arma"* and which came to

---

[62] Former Prime Minister Mehdi Frashëri was appointed Head of the Council of Regency, made up of three other councilors: Anton Harapi, friar of the Franciscan Order and representative of Albanian Catholics, Fuat Dibra, nationalist, representing the Muslim community and Lef Nosi, publisher and prominent intellectual, exponent of Orthodox Christians. The new executive was chaired by the Kosovar Rexhep Mitrovica, a strong supporter of the creation of an ethnic "Greater Albania".
[63] As Minister of Defence, Pervizi did not neglect issues relating to the security of the northern Albanian borders and visited several times the places where the two infantry regiments from the ranks of the Royal Italian Army, placed under the orders of Colonels Fuat Dibra (namesake of the aforementioned member of the Council of Regency) and Qazim Komani. The latter established the *"Kosovo National Defence Command"* in Prizren and made extensive use of volunteer troops.
[64] In September and October 1944, the partisan formations were strongly opposed by the army and other Albanian nationalist units. Since late summer the 4th Infantry Regiment has resisted with determination an offensive unleashed by Yugoslav partisans and Bulgarian forces in eastern Kosovo.
[65] The provision, issued during the government of Maliq Bushati (February - May 1943), was probably part of an Italian political conduct that was more sensitive to the requests for greater autonomy made by the Albanians. Consequently, the dissolution of the Legions of Tiranë and Vlorë and the formation of new Italian Carabinieri battalions were ordered.

include a General Command, a School, 14 higher level commands and 64 lower level commands. Also in the course of 1943 the *Albanian Border Guard* was recreated, spun off from the Italian *"Guardia di Finanza"*. Pervizi believed that the customs police units should be deployed only along the borders of the so-called "Greater Albania" and not be involved in operations conducted within the national territory. As per Albanian military tradition, the reserve continued to be fed by voluntary formations whose members were identified as *"Kreshnike"* (valiant men). These fighters could be mobilized to act as actual Border Guards if necessary or to reinvigorate already formed army units. In addition to the aforementioned forces, the Germans decided to create four battalions of Albanian militiamen[66]. Although substantially subordinated to the German military authorities, these units were formally under the control of the Albanian Minister of the Interior, the Kosovar Xhafer Deva, and were not supposed to operate outside national borders. A leading figure in the pro-German executive and an important nationalist leader, Deva is considered by several historians to be the main organizer of the violent repression carried out in Tiranë on 4 February 1944, during which numerous political opponents were eliminated. Soldiers enrolled in one of the battalions of the so-called *"Kosova"* Regiment were among the perpetrators of the massacre. The *"Kosova"* Regiment, a unit loyal to the Minister of the Interior, was considered as the armed wing of the II League of Prizren[67], an organization created in September 1943 with German approval, aimed at legitimizing the existence of an Albania made up of all the territories in which ethnic Albanian populations lived. Established thanks to the Germans in the autumn of 1943, divided into three battalions and under the orders of Colonel Bajazit Boletini, the *"Kosova"* Regiment had a strength of around 1,500 men and was used in anti-partisan operations, especially against Serbian forces. Another unit whose creation was favored by the Germans, made up of Albanians from western Macedonia, in particular from the Tetovo area (a Macedonian town part of the prefecture of Prishtine since 1941), was the *"Luboten"* Battalion[68]. The ranks of this formation, also having a motorized component, swelled over time, going from 400 to 1,200 men. Charged with protecting the ethnic Albanian population of the annexed Macedonian territories, the *"Luboten"* Battalion clashed several times with the partisans. At the end of 1943, shortly after being formed, it was sent to Kičevo to counter Yugoslav guerrillas. Some elements of the battalion had the opportunity to operate in other areas of Albania. Many irregular nationalist bands also operated alongside the Germans. In a list drawn up by the German command, 77 Albanian detachments of this type are mentioned, of different sizes, for a total of 15,600 men. The number, perhaps overestimated, is hardly refutable in the absence of an official "registry" of the pro-German bands and could include several formations of the *Balli Kombëtar*, the National Front, which will be discussed further, and various groups of *"vulnetari"*, militias assigned to the protection of local communities[69]. A similar figure also emerges from a report, most likely drawn up by Allied secret services, regarding the size of the government armed formations and pro-German military units at the beginning of May 1944, which states that the total estimated strength of the irregular bands amounted to 15,370 fighters. The document also reports that in the same period the Gendarmerie (including the School) was made up of 2,700 men and had at least

---

[66] These units were initially stationed in Pristina, Prizren, Peja (Kosovo) and Tetovo (Macedonia).
[67] The name of the organization was inspired by the First League of Prizren, founded in 1878 to protect the territorial integrity of Albania, threatened by the Treaty of San Stefano signed between Russia and Turkey which assigned Albanian lands to neighboring states.
[68] Luboten is the Albanian name of a mountain (height 2,498 m) situated on the border between Kosovo and Macedonia. The battalion thus named was formed between the end of October and the beginning of November 1943.
[69] The need to strengthen the position of the Albanian government pushed the Germans to seek more active collaboration with the nationalist armed faction. The agreement was not achieved on an ideological level but on a purely practical one. The leaders of the *Balli Kombëtar* did not have great expectations in the final German victory but were aware that only by complying with German requests they could obtain the armaments necessary to sustain the inevitable clash with the communist resistance.

four mobile battalions, the Border Guard had 1,160 soldiers (out of 1 battalion, 2 companies, 3 detachments) and the Public Security departments consisted of 500 policemen. Then, on the opposite front, partisan formations of various origins (mostly communist) were active for a total of 12,210 guerrillas and even some "autonomous" bands for a total of 3,800 men. In the spring of 1944, 4 new mobile battalions were active, also formed thanks to the contribution of German military authorities and Albanian nationalists. To face the growing threat from the communist partisans, the army had in fact tried to renew and strengthen its ranks. The III Mobile Battalion *"Vermoshi"* was created at the beginning of 1944 and included in its ranks about 200 men under the orders of Major Dod Nikolla. It was organized into 3 companies, each of which was divided into 3 platoons. In addition to elements of the Gendarmerie, it also included German small detachments and *Balli Kombëtar* formations. From 15 April to 15 September 1944, the *"Vermoshi"* Battalion was deployed in southern Albania, with the task of protecting the retreat of German forces from partisan attacks[70]. With the reconstitution of the Albanian army, ranks and insignia which were in use before 1939 were reintroduced. The colors of the collar patches were green for the Infantry, red for the Gendarmerie, purple for the Engineers and yellow for the Border Guard. The generals' patches were scarlet. Albanian infantrymen wore Italian uniforms, M33 and *"Adrian"* helmets. The Gendarmerie once again adopted the pre-war M31 uniforms characterized by straight collar and accompanied by a peaked cap[71].

▲ Soldiers of the reconstituted Albanian army taking an oath.

---

70 In June 1944 the *"Vermoshi"* Battalion fought together with the IV Mobile Battalion *"Mokra"* against communist partisans.
71 Clothing and armaments of Italian production were distributed to the *"Luboten"* Battalion.

▲ Soldiers of an Albanian infantry regiment taking an oath. Note the use of *"Adrian"* helmets. Tiranë, October 1943.

▼ The General Staff of the new Albanian army. From left to right: Major Muharrem Liku, Colonel Sami Koka (first commander of the Gendarmerie and then of the Border Guard), Lieutenant Colonel Faik Quku (senior officer of the Gendarmerie), General Prenk Pervizi (Minister of Defence), General Gustav von Myrdacz (Austrian, Chief of Staff of the Albanian Army), Colonel Hermann von Kirschner (Austrian, Inspector General of the Albanian Army).

▲ A Gendarmerie non-commissioned officer dressed in the pre-war M1931 uniform. The patches affixed to the straight collar are red (colour of the Gendarmerie). He wears a M1936 peaked-cap with a red band and the Gendarmerie frieze consisting in the Skanderbeg's helmet. The gendarme in the background wears a more recent uniform characterized by a folded collar.

▲ Two Albanian policemen photographed together with a member of the Feldgendarmerie, the German military police. The frieze on the forage caps of the two Albanians, characterized by a double-headed eagle, indicates their belonging to the public security forces.

▲ Oficers of an infantry regiment parade with the Albanian flag in front of the Germans. Tiranë, October 1943.

▼ A group made up of two Albanian policemen and two soldiers from the German Feldgendarmerie patrol the streets of Tirana.

▲ Soldiers of the *"Luboten"* Battalion accompany the coffin of a comrade during a funeral ceremony.

▼ Men and officers of the reconstituted Albanian units depicted together with some nationalist leaders. The second person sitting from the left is Kadri Cakrani, army commander in the Berat area, also known as the "Schindler of Albania" for having saved the lives of around 600 Jews. This photograph was taken in February 1944.

THE ALBANIANS IN THE WAFFEN SS

The defeat of Yugoslavia in April 1941 allowed the Germans to take over Serbia and the northern lands of Kosovo[72]. The German occupation area also comprised the eastern portion of a region known as *"Sanjak"*[73], densely inhabited by ethnic Bosnians and, to a lesser extent, Albanians, of Muslim religion. Like the Italians, the Germans had also toyed with the idea of making use of local armed groups since the second half of 1941, with the aim of countering the initiatives of the Chetniks and Yugoslav communist partisans. The Albanian and Bosnian guerrillas, united and inspired by their common religious faith, rejected any possibility of understanding with the Resistance which they perceived not only as a danger to their lands but also as a threat to the preservation of their traditions. There were therefore numerous clashes between Muslim militias and partisan and Chetnik formations. In the spring of 1941, the Germans undertook the necessary actions aimed at installing an administration favorable to them in Novi Pazar, a fundamental premise for the creation of volunteer units to be used against partisans. Subsequently, a few thousand Albanians joined the ranks of two mountain divisions of the Waffen-SS.

SS Polizei – Selbstschutz – Regiment *"Sandschak"*
1943 was a crucial year for the formation of structured local units allied to the Germans in the Balkan theater of operations. Around 6,000 ethnic Albanian fighters, of which 2,000 originally from Kosovo and 4,000 from Sanjak, were recruited by the German command in the Autumn. The bulk of these men, dressed as best they could and provided with Italian-made weapons, were used to complete the forces of a Muslim legion[74]. The unit is mentioned for the first time, in a somewhat informal manner, as *"Muselmanengruppe von Krempler"* in a document relating to an order of operations of the Waffen-SS dated 30 October 1943. The name included the surname of the first commander of the unit, as well as the main architect of the enlistment of the Sandjak Muslims, the Oberst der Polizei und Sturmbannführer der Waffen-SS Karl von Krempler. An expert in Islamic issues, Krempler was a *"Volksdeutsche"* that is, an "ethnic German" (in this specific case, he was born in Pirot, a town in south-eastern Serbia) who spoke Serbian and Turkish fluently. At the end of July 1944 the Legion was reorganized and renamed SS Polizei – Selbstschutz - Regiment *"Sandschak"* (Self-Defence Police Regiment *"Sanjak"*), divided into 4 battalions (each probably on 4 companies), with a total force that at the moment of its maximum expansion never exceeded 4,000 units. This formation fought against the partisans in Sanjak and in the eastern area of Montenegro, at least until October 1944.

---

72 As we have read, the rest of Kosovo and the neighboring territories of Montenegro and Macedonia were annexed to "Greater Albania", under Italian control, while some south-eastern areas of Kosovo and most of the lands of Macedonia were assigned to Bulgaria which joined the Tripartite Pact on 1 March 1941.
73 The term refers to a vast region between the current borders of Serbia and Montenegro, located north-west of Kosovo and south-east of Bosnia-Herzegovina. More precisely, the expression *"sanjak"* (in Turkish sancak and in Serbian санџак or sandžak) identifies a *"district"*, in other words one of the levels of the administrative subdivision of the territories belonging to the Ottoman Empire. Although originally the term indicated a first-level subdivision, with the succession of reforms aimed at modernizing the Ottoman territorial administration it ended up designating a minor district of one of the provinces of the Empire (called *"eyalet"* until 1866 and reconfigured as *"vilayet"* with a law of January 1867). In 1879 Austro-Hungarian troops invaded the Sanjak of Novi Pazar, remaining there until 1908. Once the Balkan Wars ended, with the Treaty of London in 1913 the territory was divided between Montenegro and Serbia. Until the outbreak of the Great War, at the end of which it was incorporated into the Kingdom of Yugoslavia, Sanjak became the scene of conflict between Serbs and Austro-Hungarians.
74 Some men should have received, after enlisting, German clothing and weapons. The companies were at least partly equipped with Italian support weapons.

I/28, the Albanian battalion of the 13. Waffen – Gebirgs – Division der SS *"Handschar"* (kroatische Nr. 1)

At the end of 1942 Reichsführer-SS Heinrich Himmler felt the urgency of having a greater number of troops to counter the growing threat posed by Tito's partisan forces in Yugoslavia. The results emerging from previous anthropological research conducted in Italy, which had established the Aryan origin of the Albanians and the diffusion in Croatia and Germany of similar theories with regard to the Bosnians, also legitimated from an ideological point of view the possibility of forming new Waffen-SS units enlisting young volunteers in the occupation zones. This would also have allowed the German units to be freed of territorial garrison tasks, to be profitably employed elsewhere. The first unit to be created (starting in the spring of 1943) was the 13. Waffen – Gebirgs – Division der SS *"Handschar"*[75], a mountain division made up predominantly of Bosnian Muslims which included a battalion of ethnic Albanian Muslims[76], also in this case originally from Sanjak and Kosovo, recruited to compensate for the shortage of personnel. More precisely, it was the 1st Battalion, part of the SS-Freiwilligen-Gebirgs-Jäger Regiment 2 (Kroat. Div.), in short the I/2. The Division's enlisted personnel were first sent to southern France[77] (July 1943) and subsequently in Lower Silesia[78] (October 1943) to undergo training. From the first moment the Croatian leader Ante Pavelić attempted to hinder or at least influence the realization of the German project, aimed at persuading his Bosnian subjects to join the Waffen-SS. When in July 1943 the military swore their loyalty to Hitler, political reasons led the Germans to make the Bosnians promise to also be loyal to the Poglavnik[79] and to the Independent State of Croatia. At the beginning of August 1943 the command of the Division was assumed by a Prussian, the SS-Oberführer (promoted to SS-Brigadeführer on 1 October 1943) Karl Gustav Sauberzweig. In mid-February 1944, after having completed training, the *"Handschar"* Division left Germany and was sent to Slavonia (eastern Croatia). At that time the large unit had a strength of 377 officers, 2,078 non-commissioned officers and 18,563 enlisted men while the Albanian battalion, under the orders of SS-Hauptsturmführer Walter Bormann since 1 August 1943, was made up of 18 officers, 127 non-commissioned officers and 1,340 troops[80]. Later,

---

[75] The Division took its name from a term deriving from Turkish, which indicated a short and curved Ottoman sword, known in Bosnia as handžar (handschar, the German transliteration). At first the *"Handschar"* Division was called the Kroatische SS-Freiwilligen-Gebirgs Division. At the end of the summer of 1943 the Division was formed as follows: Divisional Headquarters; 2 Mountain Infantry regiments, the SS-Freiwilligen-Gebirgs-Jäger Regiment 1 and the SS-Freiwilligen-Gebirgs-Jäger Regiment 2, both on Headquarters and, first 4, then 3 battalions (the third battalions were abolished due to personnel shortages at the time of the formation of the divisional sub-units, reconstituted in June 1944, and definitively disbanded on 31 October of the same year, given the high number of desertions); 1 Artillery regiment, the SS-Gebirgs-Artillerie Regiment 13, on 1 Headquarters and 4 battalions; 1 Reconnaissance battalion, the SS-Gebirgs-Aufklärungs Abteilung 13; 1 Anti-tank battalion, the SS-Panzerjäger Abteilung 13; an Engineer battalion, the SS-Gebirgs-Pionier Bataillon 13; 1 Anti-aircraft battalion, the SS-Flak Abteilung 13; 1 Signal battalion, the SS-Gebirgs-Nachrichten Abteilung 13; 1 Divisional transport command the SS-Divisions-Nachschubsführer 13 (transformed into SS-Versorgungs-Regiment 13, with the inclusion of all divisional services, on 24 September 1944); 1 Administrative battalion dedicated to the economic exploitation of occupied territories, the SS-Wirtschafts-Bataillon 13; 1 Medical battalion, the SS-Sanitäts-Abteilung 13. The order of battle moreover comprised 2 Cavalry squadrons, 2 Veterinary companies, 2 Mobile Workshop companies and 1 Military Police company. In the Divisional Headquarters, in all Regimental Headquarters and in all Battalions, with the exception of the Signal battalion exclusively made of German personnel, there was an Imam. Almost all of the officers were of German nationality (or Volksdeutschen). The only ethnic Albanian officer of I/28 Battalion was SS-Untersturmführer Sulejman Daca, later transferred to the 21st SS Mountain Division *"Skanderbeg"*. Reichsführer-SS Heinrich Himmler and the supreme authority of Sunni Islam, Grand Mufti Haj Amin el-Husseini visited the *"Handschar"* Division several times.

[76] In addition to Bosnian and Albanian Muslims, Albanian Catholics, Croatian Catholics, Slovenians, Germans (including the Volksdeutsche), Hungarians, Italians, and even Swiss were enrolled in the Division.

[77] The various sub-units were formed in France. In Villefranche-de-Rouergue, on 17 September 1943, an attempted mutiny occurred, orchestrated by elements close to the Yugoslav Resistance who had infiltrated the ranks of the Division.

[78] The Albanian battalion was housed in the structures of the Strans training camp, not far from the more important Neuhammer one, where the other sub-units of the Division were quartered.

[79] Poglavnik or chief was the title that identified Ante Pavelić.

[80] I/28 was divided into 6 companies. The Imam of the Albanian battalion was the Bosnian Ahmed Skaka.

the two mountain infantry regiments changed their names: they were no longer identified as 1st and 2nd but as 27th and 28th Regiments[81] and consequently the Albanian battalion, used in the first three important operations in which the Division fought, became known as I/28. From 10 to 12 March 1944 the *Unternehmen Wegweiser* took place, directed against 2,500 partisans who had chosen as their base the area around the Bosut River (a left tributary of the Sava River), covered by dense forests. Thanks to the positive outcome of the operation, the *"Handschar"* Division was able to prepare to cross the Bosnian borders according to what had been pre-arranged with the *Unternehmen Save*[82]. At dawn on March 15, I/28 was among the first units to cross the Sava River, near Brčko. The losses inflicted by the *"Titoists"*, with whom the battalion immediately came into contact, were light. On 12 April the *Unternehmen Osterei* was launched, which provided for the *"Handschar"* to continue the advance into Bosnia. The 28th Regiment moved south through the villages of Mačkovac and Priboj, east of Tuzla. The Albanians, who had the task of conquering the Majevica heights in that sector, suffered heavy losses but managed to achieve their assigned objectives. This was the last combat conducted by the battalion within the *"Handschar"* Division, since shortly after, the unit, designated as the initial nucleus of a new Waffen-SS division, was transferred by rail to Pristina[83]. Sauberzweig expressed his satisfaction with the battalion's performance, which had fought valiantly under his command. The Albanian soldiers, very close to the high-ranking Prussian officer, regretted having to leave the Division.

The 21. Waffen – Gebirgs – Division der SS *"Skanderbeg"* (albanische Nr. 1)
The Germans, recognizing the neutrality of the "Land of Eagles", wanted the pro-German government in Tiranë not to be hostile to the creation of a SS mountain division essentially made up of ethnic Albanian volunteers, the 21. Waffen – Gebirgs – Division der SS *"Skanderbeg"* (albanische Nr. 1). SS-Brigadeführer Jozef Fizthum, representative of Reichsführer-SS Heinrich Himmler in Albania, exercised the role of supervisor of the Division's training process, providing officers and non-commissioned officers to serve as instructors. In May 1944, the unit was placed under the orders of the SS-Standartenführer August Schmidhuber, born 8 May 1901 in Augsburg (Bavaria), promoted to SS-Oberführer on 21 June 1944[84]. The Albanian battalion taken from the *"Handschar"* was immediately deemed ready for combat. It was in fact a battle-proven formation, ideologically prepared, certainly suitable to represent the fulcrum of a new large unit. It was assigned as the third battalion of the second mountain infantry regiment of the *"Skanderbeg"* SS Division (the Battalion was initially called III/2 and later III/51). About two-thirds of the 11,398 volunteers recruited were Kosovar Muslims. The influx of Albanians from Albania was minor. Among Albanians there was also no shortage of Catholics. 9,275 men were considered eligible. Of these, only 6,491 were later actually enrolled. To them were added officers, non-commissioned officers and engineer, signal and other army corps specialists, mainly German, Austrian and *"Volksdeutschen"*, transferred from SS mountain infantry divisions, such as the *"Prinz Eugen"* and the *"Handschar"*. Overall the *"Skander-*

---

81 The SS Freiw. Geb. Jg. Rgt. 2 (Kroat. Div.) was redesignated Waffen-Gebirgs-Jäger Regiment der SS 28 (kroat. Nr. 2).
82 In order to solemnize the moment, Sauberzweig ordered that the commanders of the various sub-units of the Division should read a short message to the soldiers once they had passed the Sava River. This is the text:
"By crossing this river, we celebrate the great and historic task that the leader of the new Europe, Adolf Hitler, set for us: to liberate the long-suffering Bosnian homeland and, thereby, build the bridge to liberation of Muslim Albania. To our Führer, Adolf Hitler, who seeks the dawn of a just and free Europe, Sieg Heil!".
83 A new battalion was formed drawing on personnel from other sub-units of the Division and with young recruits. It is interesting to remember that other Albanians served in foreign combat units during the Second World War, especially on the Allied side. In fact, just over thirty enlisted in the French army (1939-45), the majority in the Foreign Legion. There was also no shortage of Albanians included in the French, Greek and Yugoslavian partisan ranks.
84 Interpreter for the commander of the *"Skanderbeg"* Division was the Albanian SS-Hauptsturmführer Thela Decg, from a family of landowners in southern Albania, and of an Austrian mother. Decg studied in Vienna and obtained a university degree.

beg" could count on a force of almost 9,000 men including officers, non-commissioned officers and troops. Training activities started since the Spring of 1944 were never definitively completed and the expected order of battle was therefore not achieved. Both mountain infantry regiments had to operate at reduced ranks. The Signal Battalion was only made up of two companies of telephone operators and one company of telegraph operators. The Anti-tank Battalion was probably formed with a single company equipped with 3.7 cm Pak 35/36 guns[85]. The creation of an armored component for the Albanian SS Division therefore remained on paper. The structure of the *"Skanderbeg"* Division should have been as follows:

- Divisional Headquarters
- 2 Mountain Infantry Regiments, the Waffen-Gebirgs-Jäger Regiment of the SS 50 and the Waffen-Gebirgs-Jäger Regiment der SS 51, both made up of Headquarters, 3 Battalions organized into 4 Rifle companies (1-4, 5-8, 9-12), 1 Gun company and 1 Anti-tank company
- 1 Artillery regiment, the Waffen-Gebirgs-Artillerie-Regiment der SS 21, out of 4 battalions (each on 3 batteries)
- 1 Reconnaissance battalion, the SS-Gebirgs Aufklärungs-Abteilung 21, on Headquarters and 4 companies
- 1 Anti-tank battalion, the SS-Gebirgs Panzerjäger-Abteilung 21, on Headquarters, 3 Anti-tank companies and 1 Anti-aircraft company
- 1 Engineer battalion, the SS-Gebirgs-Pionier Bataillon 21, on Headquarters and 3 companies
- 1 Signal battalion, the SS-Gebirgs-Nachrichten Abteilung 21, on Headquarters and 4 companies
- 1 Transport detachment, the SS-Versorgungs-Regiment 21, on Headquarters and 4 companies (including various divisional services)
- 1 Administrative battalion (dedicated to the economic exploitation of occupied territories), the SS-Wirtschafts-Bataillon 21, on Headquarters and 2 companies
- 1 Medical battalion, the SS-Sanitäts-Abteilung 21, on Headquarters and 2 Medical companies, 1 Field Hospital
- 1 Veterinary company

The order of battle would be completed by 1 Cavalry squadron (to be assigned to the Reconnaissance battalion) and would also include 1 Assault Gun battery.

The *"Skanderbeg"* Mountain Division was initially assigned tasks of protection and safeguarding of infrastructures, in particular the surveillance of the communication routes that connected Skopje to Mitrovica and Peja to Montenegro as well as the mines of Gjakova, Kukës and Trepça. The first actions were conducted against the partisans, despite the insufficient availability of support weapons,

---

[85] The anti-tank battalion was equipped with 3.7 cm Pak 35/36 guns. This sub-unit was probably only made up of a motorized company armed with these weapons although official sources report a more complex structure which, starting from July 1944, should have consisted of an anti-tank company, with 12 pieces of unspecified caliber (probably 7.5 cm and 5 cm guns), an anti-aircraft company, armed with 12 2 cm guns and a company equipped with 10 self-propelled guns. The actual presence of the latter, however, dates back to the last period of 1944. It would not have been a company in the strict sense but rather the Sturmgeschütz-Batterie *"Skanderbeg"*, equipped with 2 Italian M41 75/18 self-propelled guns and 8 Italian M15/42 medium tanks, transferred from Brod to Vinkovci on 20 December 1944. In fact this armored department would have been formed in conjunction with the creation of the Kampfgruppe *"Skanderbeg"*, organized with the remains of the dissolved Division in the Autumn of 1944. The Kfz 15 was the standard vehicle of the Signal battalion. According to the Tables of Organization and Equipment, at least 30 German-made vehicles of this type would have delivered to the sub-unit. Photographic evidence would demonstrate the presence of some Italian-built trucks in the divisional transport detachment.

machine guns and mortars. Subsequently, the Division had to deal with the lack of communication tools: radio equipment in particular was scarce. Real fighting took place only during the *Unternehmen Draufgänger*, an operation which took place in Montenegro in July 1944, aimed at encircling and destroying the Yugoslav partisan forces. The plan envisaged the conquest of the peaks located near Andrijevica, the occupation of Berane and the local airport, used by the Allies to supply the Resistance, and the annihilation of the formations under Tito's orders[86]. The *Unternehmen Draufgänger* ended in a fiasco for the attackers. According to August Schmidhuber, commander of the *"Skanderbeg"* Division, the difficulties posed by the terrain and the severity of the fighting forced the SS to endure enormous physical efforts. The troops of Tito, well equipped and effectively trained, behaved in combat like units of a regular army capable of holding their own against the fiercest of adversaries. The setbacks on the battlefield were followed by mass desertions which effectively decreed the dissolution of the Division[87]. According to Schmidhuber, the few units that remained intact should have formed autonomous groups tasked with exercising influence on the Albanian nationalist bands which in the meantime had moved closer to the German cause. In reality, in the autumn of 1944, what remained of the Division was reorganized into a Kampfgruppe, the vast majority of ethnic Albanian soldiers were dismissed and, at least in part, replaced with personnel from the Kriegsmarine (the German Navy). The unit, in its new configuration, was assigned to the 7. SS-Freiwilligen-Gebirgs-Division *"Prinz Eugen"* and continued to fight against the Yugoslav partisans until its final dissolution, which occurred in January 1945.

---

[86] The *"Titoist"* forces of the II Yugoslav Assault Corps were opposed, in addition to the *"Skanderbeg"* SS Division, by the 14th Regiment of the 7. Waffen - Gebirgs - Division der SS *"Prinz Eugen"*, by 3 Combat Groups, Kampfgruppen *"Bendl"*, *"Krempler"* and *"Stripel"*, elements of a *"Brandenburg"* regiment, the SS Polizei Regiment 5, Bulgarian units, Chetniks units and Albanian *"vulnetari"* formations.
[87] The reversal of alliances implemented by Bulgaria, Romania and Finland starting from the summer of 1944 reinvigorated the propaganda hostile to *"Skanderbeg"* Division. Many in Albania feared that Germany was on the verge of defeat. This state of affairs favored the phenomenon of desertions. At that time, on the border with Macedonia, as many as 1,000 soldiers abandoned the unit, taking their uniforms and weapons with them. Even the gallant battalion coming from the ranks of the *"Handschar"* Division was no exception: 697 soldiers left the unit. However, these men returned to fight a short time later. At the beginning of October 1944, the Division could count on just under 4,000 ethnic Albanian soldiers.

▲ A volunteer from I/28, the Albanian battalion of the 13th Waffen – Gebirgs – Division der SS *"Handschar"*. Armament and clothing are standard and only the headgear, clearly of Albanian origin, allows us to identify with certainty the unit to which the soldier belongs.

▲ Sergeant Rudi Sommerer and Albanian corporal Nazir Hodic, both serving in the 6. Kompanie, I/28, 13. Waffen – Gebirgs – Division der SS *"Handschar"*.

▼ Albanians from the SS Division *"Handschar"* photographed during *Unternehmen Osterei*. The radio operator is busy communicating with the command in German language.

▲ A sergeant from I/28 photographed while playing the flute in a moment of rest. After the *Unternehmen Osterei*, the Albanian *"Handschar"* battalion was transferred to the SS Mountain Division *"Skanderbeg"* which was in the process of being established.

▲ Kosovar volunteers of Albanian ethnicity enlist in the 21. Waffen – Gebirgs – Division der SS *"Skanderbeg"*. The flags of Albania, SS and Germany as well as the portraits of Skanderbeg and Adolf Hitler are visible in the background.

▼ Albanian SS from the *"Skanderbeg"* Division pictured during *Unternehmen Draufgänger*, an operation which in July 1944 aimed to destroy the *"Titoists"* partisan units deployed in Montenegro.

▲ Soldiers of the SS Mountain Division *"Skanderbeg"* foretaste a rich meal. M44 camouflage uniforms were issued to the unit in large quantities. The clothing did not always appear to be in order: some men preferred to wear bandanas on their heads instead of forage caps and their shoes were sometimes replaced to protect them from the wear and tear of the marches.

▼ Soldiers of the SS Division *"Skanderbeg"* during a pause in the fighting in July 1944. In that period the peculiar headgear introduced for the Albanians serving in the *"Handschar"* Division was no longer used.

▲ Two Albanian SS from the *"Skanderbeg"* Division eat their meal. All the men portrayed are wearing M44 camouflage uniforms.

▼ This picture shows two fighters of the Albanian volunteer militias, the so-called *"vulnetari"*, easily recognizable by the typical clothes they wear. Visible among them is a member of the SS Mountain Infantry Division *"Prinz Eugen"*. Behind them, with their camouflage uniforms, we can see two men from the SS *"Skanderbeg"* Division.

▲ *"Vulnetari"* Albanian militiamen photographed together with soldiers of the SS Division *"Prinz Eugen"*.

RESISTANCE AND CIVIL WAR

Since 1941 small detachments of partisans began to harass Italian patrols in Albanian territory. Organized into local militias, the Albanian resistance recorded its first encouraging successes in the first half of 1942. On 16 September of that year, the Communists convened a conference which was also open to the Royalist and Nationalist forces. Thus the *"Lufta Nacional Çlirimtare"* (National Liberation Movement) was established, a body that brought together all the factions that opposed the Italian occupation. The Communist Party of Albania had in fact set itself the task of creating a national liberation army since March 1943. The prospect of the creation of a "Greater Albania", supported first by Italy and then by Germany, rekindled the aspirations of that segment of the population most sensitive to calls of a nationalist nature. The *Balli Kombëtar*[88] ,that is, the National Front, which fought against Italians and Germans[89], considered Yugoslavia and Greece to be bitter enemies of the Shqiptars. The Nationalists believed that Kosovo should be an integral part of the Albanian nation at the end of the conflict while the Communists rejected such a hypothesis and aimed to preserve the solid understanding that united them to the Yugoslav partisan movement. In the Summer of 1943 the Albanian regular partisan forces already numbered around 10,000 fighters organized into more than 20 battalions. At least another 20,000 volunteers were grouped in territorial detachments operating in occupied areas. In July 1943 the General Council of the *"Lufta Nacional Çlirimtare"* set up a General Staff of the Liberation Army, appointing Enver Hoxha as political commissioner of the same[90]. After the Mukaj Conference held from 1 to 3 August 1943, in which the delegates of the *Balli Kombëtar* put forward a proposal having as its object the dissolution of the General Council and the creation of a new committee for the salvation of Albania, the split between Communists and Nationalists became incurable. The Communists opposed this project and consequently the *"Lufta"* took on an undeniable leading role in the fight for the liberation of the "Land of Eagles". However, the unity of the resistance front ended up shattering and shortly thereafter an open armed struggle began, destined to turn into a civil war. According to a German estimate, in October 1943 the Albanian National Front could count on a total strength of around 8,000 men. At the beginning of 1944, around twenty battalions of the *Balli Kombëtar* were employed alongside the Germans against the communist partisans. The units of the Albanian National Liberation Army, pressed by the enemy, had to face a harsh winter, retreating to the mountains. A new anti-partisan offensive promoted by the Germans in May 1944 ended in failure.

During 1942, in Macedonia, a small unit of ethnic Albanian guerrillas was formed under the orders of Xhemë Hasa, operating in the area between Gostivar and Tetovo[91]. Hasa's resistance was of a patri-

---

[88] Political and military organization founded in 1939 by Mid'hat Frasheri (writer and political exponent, cousin of Mehdi) aimed at the reunification of all the territories inhabited by ethnic Albanian populations in a single State. The first nationalist groups arose in Vlorë, Skrapar, Kolonje and Tirana. *Balli Kombëtar* committees spread throughout Kosovo before the end of 1942.

[89] The National Front fought the Italians from the end of 1942 until the Armistice. One of the best-known clashes was the one which saw the participation of the nationalist *"Shqiponja"* (Eagle) Battalion, supported by a communist formation in Gjorm, between December 1942 and January 1943. Among the other battles conducted by the armed units of the *Balli Kombëtar* against Italian troops in Albania can be remembered the following fightings: Greshicë (Mallakastër, February 1943), Ruzhdie (March 1943), Selenicë (April 1943), Gjinaqar (June 1943), Vasjar (June 1943), Humelicë (August 1943), Berat (August 1943), Reç (August 1943), Dukat (Vlorë, August 1943), Këlcyrë (September 1943), Gërhot (Gjirokastër, September 1943). Nationalist forces faced the Germans primarily in the late Summer and early Autumn of 1943.

[90] Enver Hoxha was born on 16 October 1908 in Gjirokastër and educated at the University of Montpellier. In France, the young Enver associated with intellectuals and politicians who convinced him to adhere to the Marxist ideology. From 1934 to 1936 he worked at the Albanian consulate in Brussels. Military commander of the Albanian National Liberation Army was Spiro Moisiu, known as Spiro Koxhobashi at the time when he was commander of the *"Tomori"* Battalion.

[91] The small formation (about 1,000 men) was incorporated into the structure of the *Balli Kombëtar* in western Macedonia.

otic nature: the primary objective was the expulsion of the foreign occupier, wherever he came from. After the occupation of Gostivar by the Italians, the Albanian leader placed himself at their service to best protect the interests of the inhabitants of those lands, with an anti-Yugoslav function. Already in the spring of 1943, pressured by important exponents of the local nationalist camp, he nevertheless decided to also take sides against his allies. The Albanian partisan command then attempted to convince Hasa to cooperate for the liberation of Gostivar. In the absence of clear assurances on the role that would be assigned to the representatives of the ethnic Albanian population in the Macedonian political structure once the war was over, Hasa rejected any offer of collaboration. The men under his command fought against the Chetniks, the Yugoslav partisans and the Albanian National Liberation Army. The composite panorama made up of the factions fighting for the liberation of Albania was completed by the Monarchists (Zogists) and other nationalist groups not affiliated with the *Balli Kombëtar*. *Legaliteti* was the political movement that supported the return of King Zog as head of an independent ethnic "Greater Albania". It was established on 21 November 1943 with Ndoc Çoba, former Albanian Finance Minister, as president and Abaz Kupi, who distinguished himself in the fighting in Durrës in 1939, as military leader. At the time of its formation *Legaliteti* had 25,000 members, of whom at least 5,000 were armed. Particularly active in the regions of Tiranë, Shkodër, Dibër, Durrës, Vlorë and Korça, as well as in Kosovo, this minior monarchist faction managed to establish relations with the Communists but especially with the other nationalist movements and obtained the support of an allied mission [92]. *Legaliteti* leaders mainly came from the officer ranks of Zog's army. In the Summer of 1944 the movement practically ceased to exist. Small independent nationalist groups operated in northern Albania. The most important were those led by Gani Bey Kryeziu and Colonel Muharrem Bajraktari. Kryeziu, born in Kosovo, was former aide-de-camp to Alexander I of Yugoslavia. After the Italian occupation of Albania he joined the Albanian resistance, working to create a united front in order to avert the hegemonic aims of Monarchists and Communists. At the end of 1943 he managed to deploy 500 men against the Germans. At the beginning of the summer of 1944 the number of personnel under his command doubled. Kryeziu was constantly supported by the British but the inconsistency of forces under him and the hostility towards other partisan movements inevitably marked the end of his armed movement. Albanian Colonel Muharrem Bajraktari mobilized about 1,000 guerrillas in Lumës Province. Arguably the most colorful of nationalist leaders, Bajraktari believed he embodied Albania's future and aimed to convince London that there was no serious alternative to his leadership. An example of the singular attitude of the Albanian colonel can be found in a report sent in January 1944 to Anthony Eden, Secretary of State for Foreign Affairs of the Churchill government, in which it was argued that Albania would be crucial for the future of British policy in the Balkans in an anti-Slavic and anti-communist perspective. Bajraktari also told the British that he was able to foment an uprising against the Germans in exchange for weapons and money. These were clearly projects completely divorced from reality. After having participated in the founding of the *Legaliteti* movement, the colonel stipulated a sort of non-aggression pact with the Germans which he however decided to break in August 1944. Despite the leaders of the Albanian resistance ordering him to collaborate more assiduously with other partisan units, under penalty of death, Bajraktari preferred to return to the mountains.

At the beginning of Autumn 1944, the command of the Albanian National Liberation Army developed the plan to liberate Tiranë which involved the annihilation of the German units present in the Elbasan - Durrës- Kruja area and the commitment of 11 Partisan Assault Brigades. The decisive attack was launched in the early hours on 16 November 1944. The following day the capital was free.

92 In the period between the spring of 1943 and the end of 1944, approximately 50 of His Majesty's officers were sent to Albania. The first British launches to the Shqiptar resistance began on 17 April 1943. In September 1944, having taken note of the effective dissolution of the Zogist and nationalist armed groups, the Foreign Office decided to exclusively support the communist partisans of the Albanian National Liberation Army, the only force that was effectively fighting the Germans at that time.

▲ Young guerrillas of the Albanian National Front on board trucks. The *Balli Kombëtar* movement comprised an armed youth organization whose groups clashed with both the Chetniks and the partisans of the *"Lufta Nacional Çlirimtare"*.

▲ Fighters of the *Balli Kombëtar*. These men wear a mix of clothes of civil and military origin but on their heads they all wear a *qeleshe* adorned with a red shield inside which the black double-headed eagle of Albania stands out.

▼ Major Peter Kemp (third from left), member of an Allied mission to the Albanian resistance, is portrayed here between two other British officers together with partisans. Note that the patriots could belong to a formation linked to the monarchist *Legaliteti* movement since one of them salutes in the Zogist manner, with the right hand placed at the height of the heart and the palm of the same facing downwards. Vicinity of Dibër, November 1943.

▲ Armed men of the *Balli Kombëtar* listen to a speech by Xhafer Deva, Minister of the Interior of the pro-German Albanian government.

▲ The man who appears in the foreground in this photograph is Abaz Kupi, head of the *Legaliteti* movement.

THE ALBANIAN NATIONAL LIBERATION ARMY

The most representative unit of the communist-led Albanian National Liberation Army was the Assault Brigade, generally made up of 4 battalions (minimum 3, maximum 5) and 1 Heavy Weapons Company. Sometimes it included one or more artillery batteries, a mortar company and reconnaissance and liaison units (usually with 3 or 4 squads), a structure similar to that of the Yugoslav Partisan Brigade. Initially the Albanian brigade included around 400 - 600 men but over time the numbers could expand, reaching and even exceeding the figure of 800 - 1,000 fighters. Each battalion was usually divided into 3 or 4 companies, each with around 150-200 fighters. Each company was divided into 4 or 5 squads of 50-70 men. Partisan groups had also been formed bringing together various battalions and territorial squads, directed by area commands. Practically at every level there was a command with military commander, political commissioner and related deputies. The Albanian National Liberation Army mobilized 24 Assault Brigades:

1st Assault Brigade
It was formed on 15 August 1943 and was immediately thrown into the fray by opposing the enemy at Mallakastër in November and at Mesaplik in December. In the months of February and March 1944 it was employed against German units and *Balli Kombëtar* formations. It later contributed to the liberation of Pogradec together with the 4th Assault Brigade. In September 1944 the 1st Brigade fought for the liberation of Kruja. Between October and November 1944 the unit participated in the actions aimed at liberating Tiranë. The position of Brigade Commander was assumed by Mehmet Shehu, a veteran of the Spanish War in the Republican ranks. Initially the 1st Brigade had 558 partisans distributed across 4 battalions, 1 mortar company, 1 anti-tank company, 1 artillery battery. Later the Italians of the *"Gramsci"* Battalion were added to its order of battle.

2nd Assault Brigade
It was created on 28 November 1943 with partisans coming mainly from the areas of Tiranë, Elbasan, Gjirokastër and Berat. It had a strength of 450 men distributed across 3 battalions. It suffered heavy losses during the offensive launched by the enemy in the winter of 1943-44. In April 1944 it was then transferred to the Korça region to be reorganized. The Brigade later opposed the Germans and nationalist forces. It liberated Leskovik, Ersekë, Korça and Bilishti.

3rd Assault Brigade
Formed near Tiranë on 9 October 1943, it had 379 men in 3 battalions, a 75/13 artillery battery and an 81 mm mortar company. It also operated against pro-German Albanian forces. Reduced in ranks, in February 1944 it reached a strength of around 500 men. After a few months of rest, the 3rd Brigade resumed fighting in August, clashing with German, nationalist and *Legaliteti* formations in the vicinity of Elbasan and Tiranë. In October 1944 this partisan unit entered Kosovo and at the end of November moved in the direction of Sanjak.

4th Assault Brigade
It was created on 28 December 1943. It included 550 men in 4 battalions. The 4th Brigade fought near Korça, Tiranë, Durrës and Shkodër. It collaborated with Mehmet Shehu's 1st Brigade to conquer Pogradec. After the liberation of Tiranë its partisans marched on Shkodër.

5th Assault Brigade
It was established on 20 January 1944 with 960 partisans in 5 battalions. The original nucleus of this unit consisted of 3 battalions and was formed on 28 November 1943. During its operational life it faced German forces and Zogist formations of the *Legaliteti* movement. The unit took part in the liberation of the province of Dibër together with the 18th Assault Brigade. On 1 October 1944 it moved to Kosovo to collaborate with the 1st and 4th Kosovar Brigades of the Yugoslav Liberation Army. During his stay in Kosovo his ranks were replenished by local partisans and by a battalion of Italian fighters. The 5th Brigade was thus able to have approximately 2,000 men. It was also reinforced with a mountain battery equipped with 6 75/13 pieces, captured near Prizren. It caused considerable losses to the enemy.

6th Assault Brigade
Formed on 26 January 1944 in Permeti with 912 men, at a time when the enemy's winter offensive had reached its maximum intensity. It included partisan battalions from the Gjirokastër region.

7th Assault Brigade
It was created on 17 March 1944 with 420 fighters distributed in 3 battalions. From June to September the Brigade was engaged in numerous battles and in October it took action to liberate Shkodër. After clearing northern Albania of the nationalists of the *Balli Kombëtar* and of the forces of Muharrem Bajraktari, the 7th Assault Brigade fought against the Germans from 12 December 1944 to 7 February 1945 in Montenegro, Kosovo, Macedonia, Sanjak and Bosnia. During the last phase of the conflict, it numbered 1,200 partisans in 6 battalions.

8th Assault Brigade
It was formed on April 25, 1944 with 850 partisans ordered in 4 battalions. In the Summer of 1944 it fought to liberate Gjirokastër. It then collaborated with the 16th Assault Brigade to free Lushnje and was also employed in the battle of Tiranë. The Brigade also engaged in various battles in Montenegro.

9th Assault Brigade
Divided into 4 battalions, it was born on 16 October 1944. It participated in the liberation of Korça in collaboration with the 2nd and 20th Assault Brigades. It inflicted heavy casualties on the enemy and seized large quantities of materials.

10th Assault Brigade
It was formed on 6 November 1944 with 1,225 men divided into 4 battalions. The 10th Brigade took part in the operations for the conquest of Tiranë causing serious losses in men and equipment to the enemy.

11th Assault Brigade
It was established in the liberated city of Fieri on 1 November 1944 with fighters belonging to 3 battalions of the Mallakastër Group and one battalion of the Myzeke Group. Its 1,200 partisans were divided into 4 battalions. On 11 November, in conjunction with the 12th Assault Brigade, it successfully attacked a German column near Peqin. The unit participated in the liberation of Durazzo and also had the opportunity to operate against Albanian nationalist groups.

12th Assault Brigade
It was created on 20 May 1944 with 4 battalions and had an overall strength of 650 men. It was active along the Ionian and Adriatic coasts and in the areas of Vlorë and Peqin.

14th Assault Brigade
It was formed on 17 August 1944 with 559 men in 3 battalions and a heavy weapons platoon. The arrival of new volunteers allowed the formation of a fourth battalion in September 1944. This unit fought to liberate Gjirokastër, Sarandë and other cities in southern Albania.

15th Assault Brigade
It was established on 29 June 1944 with 750 partisans from the battalions operating near Korça. It fought in the areas of Korça, Elbasan and Pogradec, cities liberated by the Brigade; in the Pogradec gorge it collided with elements of the *Balli Kombëtar* and German units. It took part in the operations for the liberation of Tiranë. In November 1944 the strength of this formation amounted to approximately 1,200 men.

16th Assault Brigade
It was formed with 456 partisans on 20 August 1944 through the incorporation of 1 battalion from Berat and 2 battalions from Mallakastër, and the arrival of volunteers from the Lushnje area. The force expanded with the creation of a fourth battalion on 10 September 1944. It was employed in the Berat - Vlorë - Lushnje area and set daring ambushes on enemy columns. Together with the III Partisan Group of Mallakastër it liberated Fieri on 15 October 1944. Subsequently the Brigade gave his contribution to the liberation of Lushnje.

17th Assault Brigade
It was formed on 26 September 1944 with 700 fighters organized into 3 battalions. It clashed with pro-German Albanian armed groups. It was used in the operations to conquer Tiranë. Later the formation operated in Macedonia.

18th Assault Brigade
It was created on 20 August 1944, divided into 4 battalions. It fought against the Germans and the nationalists. Its partisans liberated Dibër together with the 5th Brigade. On 5 November 1944, the 18th Assault Brigade attacked the Germans at Kukës. It took part in the liberation of Prizren on 16 November 1944.

19th Assault Brigade
Formed on 30 August 1944 with the *"Thoma Lula"*, *"Thanos Ziko"* and *"Pandeli Bocari"* Battalions, it had a total of 800 partisans. It was active against German units and formations of the *Balli Kombëtar*. This unit contributed to the liberation of Gjirokastër, Sarandë and Delvinë.

20th Assault Brigade
Its establishment dates back to 9 September 1944. On 30 October of that same year it organized an ambush on German troops moving on the railway Kukës- Elbasan. The latter city was liberated by this Brigade.

22nd Assault Brigade
It was born on 18 September 1944 with 1,100 fighters divided into 4 battalions. This Brigade liberated Shkodër and continued to fight in Montenegro and Bosnia.

23rd Assault Brigade
It was formed on 21 September 1944 with 700 men. It was divided into 3 battalions. It participated in the operations to liberate Tiranë. On 1 November 1944 the Brigade freed Kruja and then took

part in the capture of Shkodër. It also fought in Montenegro together with the 7th and 24th Assault Brigades.

24th Assault Brigade
At the time of its formation it had around 650 partisans. The Brigade comprised fighters from a battalion of the Lumës area and volunteers from the Kukës area. Thanks to these forces 4 battalions were activated. From 31 October to 7 November 1944 it ran over the retreating German columns on the Kukës-Prizren road and from 10 November 1944 it took part in the battle to liberate the Albanian capital.

25th Assault Brigade
It was formed on 6 November 1944 with 3 battalions and some territorial detachments. It liberated some regions of Montenegro and advanced towards Sanjak and Bosnia. This formation collaborated with the Yugoslav II Korpus in the liberation of Priepolje.

27th Assault Brigade
It was created on 29 November 1944 in Shkodër and boasted a strength of 1,200 men. It liberated some places in Montenegro and in particular Podgorica, in collaboration with Yugoslav partisan units.

Usually, 3 or 4 Brigades were grouped into Divisions[93]. In turn, 2 or 3 Divisions formed an Army Corps (Korparmata).
The armament of the partisan formations of the Albanian National Liberation Army included various models of rifles and machine guns. These weapons were most frequently those that made up the German, Italian and British equipment[94]. With the capitulation of Italy, the partisans were able to get their hands on large quantities of arms and ammunition. Each rifle squad had at least one light machine gun and each company was armed with a heavy machine gun. The artillery essentially consisted of 75/13 mountain howitzers, 65/17 pieces, 47/32 Italian anti-tank guns, and mortars of various calibers, mainly 45 and 81 millimeters. During the second phase of the partisan war, the Albanian National Liberation Army managed to deploy around 180 guns, often decentralized in support of the individual battalions. However, artillery tractors were rare. In the final stages of the battle for the liberation of Tiranë, the communist partisans managed to put a couple of unspecified armored vehicles back into operation which were used in the fightings against the Germans. The clothing of the partisans, at least in the early periods of the struggle, was a mix of civilian clothes and items of military origin, especially Italian, Yugoslavian and German. As time passed, the Albanian patriots took on an appearance more and more similar to that of their counterparts in other European countries thanks also to the Allied supplies, consisting above all in the characteristic British Battledresses. At the end of the war, rather elaborate ranks also appeared, very similar to those applied on the uniforms of the Yugoslav partisans. The headdresses of various origins, worn by the fighters of the Liberation Army, were often embellished with red stars sometimes complete with hammer and sickle.

---

93 At least 6 Assault Divisions of the Albanian National Liberation Army were established.
94 The Albanian partisans used Bren submachine guns, Breda machine guns, German machine guns (MG 34 and MG 42) and British anti-tank rifles (the well-known Boys). The *"Titoists"* also provided the Shqiptar fighters with a fair number of British Lee Enfield rifles.

▲ A 75/13 pack howitzer of the 3rd Assault Brigade. The artillery of this formation was the protagonist of an episode today remembered by a monument erected on the Sauk hill: on 18 October 1943, a 75/13 piece served by an Italian artilleryman and two Albanian partisans hit the Royal Palace in Tiranë, where the representatives of the pro-German regime had gathered.

▼ A 75/13 howitzer of an Albanian partisan battery opens fire against the enemy.

▲ Group photo of Albanian partisans from the Mallakastër district probably dating back to 1943.

▼ The men of the allied missions were often present in the largest partisan formations. This photograph was taken on the occasion of the establishment of the 8th Assault Brigade of the Albanian National Liberation Army.

▲ Enver Hoxha, political commissioner of the General Staff of the Liberation Army.

▼ Baba Faja Martaneshi, mystic of the Islamic Sufi Bektashi brotherhood and partisan leader, was co-founder and member of the National Liberation Movement. The cleric is armed with a Thompson submachine gun. This photograph dates back to October 1943.

▲ The war flag of an Albanian partisan formation.

▲ The support weapons of the 22nd Assault Brigade. This formation was created rather late, only two months before the liberation of Tiranë.

▼ Albanian partisans with a German MG 42 of war prize.

▲ Enver Hoxha photographed during the days of the Permeti Congress (24-28 May 1944) which sanctioned the birth of a provisional government.

▲ Mehmet Shehu, commander of the 1st Assault Brigade, photographed on an L6 light tank. The armored vehicle has the typical Italian markings and could therefore have been used by soldiers of the Royal Italian Army integrated into the ranks of the Albanian resistance.

▼ Partisans from the 12th Assault Brigade. Formed with 650 men, in November 1944 the strength of this unit had doubled.

▲ Enver Hoxha among the soldiers belonging to the protection department of the General Staff of the Albanian National Liberation Army. Some men wear British clothing.

▲ This image shows a German self-propelled gun, obtained by placing a 20 mm anti-aircraft piece in the bed of a truck, put out of action by the Albanian partisans in November 1944, a few days before the liberation of Tiranë.

▼ Tiranë has now been liberated and some partisans examine the turret of a German light tank installed on a fixed defensive position.

▲ Albanian partisans take over the headquarters of Radio Tirana (17 November 1944).

▼ Another shot taken after the liberation of the Albanian capital. Note the weapon in the hand of the first partisan from the right, a British-made Boys anti-tank rifle.

▲ Albanian partisans pose in the liberated capital.

▼ The partisans of the Albanian National Liberation Army parade in Tiranë on 28 November 1944 to celebrate the victory over the Germans.

▲ Three Albanian partisans pose in front of a road sign indicating the entrance to Tiranë. The first from the left is armed with a Mannlicher-Schönauer Y1903 rifle (produced for the Greek army by Steyr Mannlicher), the one in the center with an Italian Carcano 91 musket. The patriot on the right is probably armed with a Mauser rifle (M1924 or M1930) produced in Belgium by Fabrique National.

▲ German anti-tank guns captured by Albanian partisans, towed by trucks through the streets of Tirana on 28 November 1944: on the left a PaK 40 (7.5 cm caliber), on the right a PaK 38 (5 cm caliber). This latest artillery piece is towed by an initial production British Bedford MWD light truck. Red stars were painted on the bodies of the vehicles.

▼ The howitzer of the *"Cotta"* Battery, transported by truck, photographed during the Tiranë parade. Note the red star painted on the bottom left of the vehicle bed. It is the same symbol that appears on the back of the vehicles used to tow the German anti-tank guns visible in one of the previous photos.

ITALIAN SOLDIERS IN ALBANIAN RESISTANCE

The *"Firenze"* Infantry Division (127th and 128th Infantry Regiment and 41st Artillery Regiment) was not surprised by the Armistice and remained united at the orders of General Arnaldo Azzi, positioned in the Dibër region. Other disbanded soldiers reached the large unit just at the moment in which its commander was seeking an agreement with the Albanian partisans[95]. The Italians occupied the city of Kruja which was however reconquered by the Germans after fierce fighting on 28 September 1943. With the defeat the *"Firenze"* Division did not dissolve completely but was divided into smaller departments to better adapt to the conduct of guerrilla warfare alongside the battalions of the Albanian National Liberation Army. The fate of other Italian divisions stationed in Albania was different. Many soldiers of the *"Brennero"*, *"Parma"*, *"Puglie"*, *"Arezzo"* and *"Perugia"* Divisions were disarmed and captured by the Germans. In the frantic days that followed 8 September 1943, Lieutenant Colonel Mario Barbi Cinti, commander of Shijak airport, developed the idea of going up into the mountains with some soldiers, thus giving impetus to the birth of the Italian Mountain Troop Command, the C.I.T. a. M. (Comando Italiano Truppe alla Montagna). On 17 September 1943 the 1st Battalion of the C.I.T. a. M. was formed, organized around Headquarters and three companies. It was Barbi Cinti's intention to place the Italian troops still capable of fighting under a single command. On 29 September 1943 General Azzi was appointed commander of the C.I.T. a. M. which was immediately divided into 9 military zones. In mid-October 1943 the zones were configured as follows:

Peza military zone
A battalion of 300 men depended on it under the command of Lieutenant Colonel Goffredo Zignani. This unit was created on 3 October 1943 through the merger of two independent companies of 150 soldiers each, the *"Morelli"* Battalion (750 men), the *"Mosconi"* Battalion[96] (450 men) and a formation of 43 men commanded by Colonel Coviello. Around 40 soldiers from the *"Arezzo"* Division, the 5th Battery of the 41st *"Firenze"* Artillery Regiment and a group of 12 men with a 47/32 anti-tank gun were assigned to the 3rd Albanian Assault Brigade.

Dajti military zone
The 1st Battalion of the 127th *"Firenze"* Infantry Regiment (just over 400 soldiers), the support battery of the aforementioned battalion (without artillery pieces and with 69 men), a department formed by the 41st Artillery Regiment Headquarters and elements of a Border Guard (Guardia alla Frontiera) Machine Gun Battalion were under this command.

Berat military zone
It included 1 training battalion made up of the XIII Border Guard Group (150 men), 1 Autonomous Company made up of the 1525th 20 mm Battery (120 men), plus another training battalion (about 150 men). The bulk of the unarmed soldiers came from the ranks of the *"Monferrato"* Cavalry Regiment.

Dibra military zone
Dependent on it were a small training department (40 men) under the command of 2nd Lieutenant Frasce of the *"Brennero"* Division and 1,250 unarmed men employed as workers. With the arrival of General Piccini who became commander of this zone, the *"Dibra"* Battalion, composed of 300

---
95 Haxhi Lleshi, member of the General Staff of the Albanian National Liberation Army, collaborated with the veterans of the *"Firenze"* Division from the first days following 8 September, endorsing Azzi's request not to give up their weapons in order to turn them against the Germans, contrary to what a British mission required.
96 The *"Mosconi"* Battalion was born from the 104th Heavy Vehicle Group.

men reinforced by a 65/17 battery and an 81 mm mortar platoon, was established on 28 September 1943[97].

Elbasan military zone
It included a training battalion named *"Nuova Italia"* (300 men mostly from the *"Arezzo"* Division), a training company with 150 Carabinieri, mainly coming from the *"Gamucci"* Column[98]. Other units were attached to various Albanian partisan brigades: the *"Gramsci"* Battalion (170 men), the 6th and 9th Batteries of the 41st Artillery Regiment and a pack mule unit of the *"Firenze"* Division were with the 1st Assault Brigade, while the 7th Battery of the 41st Artillery Regiment was assigned to the 3rd Assault Brigade.

Vlorë military zone
Only around 1,500 Italian soldiers in poor physical condition, poorly equipped and without armament (mostly infantrymen, artillerymen and Carabinieri of the *"Parma"* and *"Perugia"* Divisions) depended on this command.

Mathi military zone
About 300 completely unarmed men depended on this area.

Korça military zone
The situation of the soldiers present in this zone is not known.

Gjirokastër military zone
The presence of armed Italian units dependent on this command has not been ascertained.

Probably considered as the most famous Italian unit that participated in the liberation of Albania, the *"Gramsci"* Battalion was largely made up of soldiers from the *"Firenze"* Division which in October 1943 separated from the column under the command of Major Martino, returning from the battle of Kruja, accepting Mehmet Shehu's proposal to become an integral part of the 1st Assault Brigade. Placed at the command of Terzilio Cardinali, the Italians concentrated in an autonomous battalion. Cardinali fell on 8 July 1944 and was replaced by his deputy, Giuseppe Monti. In mid-October 1944 the *"Gramsci"* had 278 men in 1 command platoon and 3 companies. The Battalion took part in the liberation of Tiranë. As more men arrived at the unit, Mehmet Shehu suggested the formation of a fourth company. Expanded in strength and transformed into a partisan division, the fighters of the *"Gramsci"* returned to Italy on 26 May 1945. Different from that of the *"Firenze"* Division was the fate of the *"Perugia"* Infantry Division whose soldiers were largely captured by the Germans. The 81 mm Mortar Company of the 129th *"Perugia"* Infantry Regiment, under the command of Lieutenant Celestino, gave birth to a formation that would be attached to the 5th Battalion of the 5th Albanian Assault Brigade. At the end of November 1944 the unit, in which other Italian soldiers were collected, transformed into the VI Battalion of the aforementioned Brigade[99]. In April 1945 the unit took the name of an officer killed in combat, being renamed *"Carlo Palumbo"*. Two Italian formations

---

97 The *"Dibra"* Battalion was disbanded on 12 June 1944.
98 Over 100 Carabinieri from a column also made up of infantrymen, Blackshirts and elements of the Guardia di Finanza were killed by a formation of Albanian partisans on 4 November 1943.
99 At the time of the formation of the battalion of the 5th Assault Brigade, only the *"Gramsci"* Battalion and the 2 batteries of the 41st *"Firenze"* Artillery Regiment were operational: the 6th Battery and the 9th Battery. The 6th Battery destroyed two German light self-propelled guns during the Battle of Kruja. Like the *"Gramsci"* Battalion, this battery was later integrated into the 1st Albanian Assault Brigade. The 9th Battery operated with a single piece for almost the entire duration of the war of liberation of Albania.

lined up alongside the Albanian partisans bore the name of the socialist deputy Giacomo Matteotti: the Çeta[100] *"Matteotti"* and the *"Matteotti"* Battalion. The first originated from a group of 50 Italian soldiers who presented themselves at the command of the *"Dajti"* partisan battalion, the second had a force of 60 men equipped only with individual weapons. The *"Risorgimento"* Company was formed on the initiative of 2nd Lieutenant De Julio on 13 September 1943 around a small group of officers and tankmen from the II Armored Cavalry Squadron *"Alessandria"*, totaling 50 men. Organized into 2 platoons of 3 squads (of 8 men each), the small unit was aggregated to the Albanian partisan battalion *"Dajti"*. At the end of September, a few days after having freed 750 Italian soldiers destined for prison[101], the department was incorporated into the *"Nuova Italia"* partisan battalion, which was in the process of being established. In the Autumn of 1943 the *"Fratelli Bandiera"* Company was formed. The 47 men who composed this formation were Italian soldiers who were hosted by Albanian families to perform work. This small unit became the 3rd Company of the Albanian Battalion *"Reshit Çollaku"*. Under the date of 22 October 1943, the *"Autonomous Platoon of Pogradec"* was operational, with 1 officer and 30 soldiers. The 6th Artillery Battery of Captain Vito Menegazzi and the 9th Artillery Battery of Captain Filippo Cotta, both of the 41st Artillery Regiment of the *"Firenze"* Division, equipped with 75/13 pieces, were placed directly under the Albanian partisan command. The other two surviving batteries from the same regiment, the 5th commanded by Lieutenant Ezio Giannoni and the 7th under the orders of Lieutenant Franco Sainati, were respectively assigned to support the 3rd and 5th Albanian Assault Brigades. Captain Fantacci's 81 mm Mortar Section was instead attached to Mehmet Shehu's Brigade immediately after the Kruja fighting. It later operated in support of various other partisan formations according to contingent operational needs.

▲ Tiranë, 28 November 1944: fighters of the *"Gramsci"* Battalion participate in the victory parade. Some of them wear British uniforms.

---

100 Translatable as company, department, detachment.
101 These soldiers later formed the *"Morelli"* Battalion.

BIBLIOGRAPHY

Much of the material used for the realization of this publication was obtained from documentation preserved in Albanian, British, Italian, American and German archives. Therefore, only books that can be of useful consultation for those wishing to delve deeper into the topics covered in these pages are cited below.

Amery Julian, *"Sons of the Eagle: A Study in Guerilla War"*, Hailer Publishing, Saint Petersburg, 2005.

"Annuario del Regno d'Albania", Casa Editrice Ravagnati, Milan, 1940.

Battistelli Pier Paolo, *"The Balkans 1940-41 (1) – Mussolini's Fatal Blunder in the Greco-Italian War"*, Osprey Publishing, Oxford, 2021.

Biagini Antonello, *"Storia dell'Albania: dalle origini ai giorni nostri"*, Bompiani, Milan, 1998.

Bishop Chris, *"SS Hitler's Foreign Divisions – Foreign Volunteers in The Waffen-SS 1940-45"*, Spellmount, Staplehurst, 2005.

Cappellano Filippo, Orlando Salvatore, *"L'Esercito Italiano dall'Armistizio alla Guerra di Liberazione: 8 settembre 1943-25 aprile 1945"*, Ufficio Storico Stato Maggiore dell'Esercito, Rome, 2005.

Crippa Paolo, *"Italian Armored Units in the Balkans 1941-1945"*, Soldiershop Publishing, Zanica, 2019.

Crippa Paolo, Manes Luigi, "Italy 43-45 – AFVs and MVs of co-belligerent units", Mattioli 1885, Fidenza, 2018.

Crociani Piero, *"Gli Albanesi nelle Forze Armate Italiane 1939-1943"*, Ufficio Storico Stato Maggiore dell'Esercito, Rome, 2001.

Crociani Piero, *"Albanesi in grigioverde"*, Storia Modellismo Anno V n. I, pp. 25-28, Orion Editrice, Rome, 1981.

Crociani Piero, Battistelli Pier Paolo, *"Italian Blackshirt 1935-45"*, Osprey Publishing, Oxford 2010.

Cuzzi Marco, *"Quando Mussolini costruiva la Grande Albania"*, Macedonia/Albania le terre mobili, Limes N.2/01, Gruppo Editoriale L'Espresso, Rome, 2001.

Di Colloredo Mels Pierluigi Romeo, *"Per vincere ci vogliono i leoni…i fronti dimenticati delle Camicie Nere 1939-1943"*, Soldiershop Publishing, Zanica, 2019.

Dingu Kadri, *"Lufta Antifashiste Nacional Çlirimtare: Epopeja e Lavdishme e Popullit Shqiptar"*, Arian, Tiranë, 2001.

Dželetović Ivanov Pavle, *"21. SS-divizija Skenderbeg"*, Nova knjiga, Belgrade, 1987.

Fischer Bernd, *"Albania at War 1939-1945"*, Purdue University Press, London, 1999.

Frasheri Kristo, *"Mbi historinë e Ballit Kombëtar"*, Botimet Dudaj, Tiranë, 2012.

Hidri Pietër, *"Gjeneral Prenk Pervizi"*, Botimet Toena, Tiranë, 2002.

Instituti i studimeve Marksiste-Leniniste Pranë KQ të PPSH, Instituti i Historisë Pranë Akademisë së Shkencave të RPSSH, Arkivi I Qendror i PPSH, *"Epopeja e Luftes Antifashiste Nacional Çlirimtare e Popullit Shqiptar 1939-1944"*, Shtëpia Botuese 8 Nëntoru, Tiranë, 1980.

Lepre George, *"Himmler's Bosnian Division: The Waffen-SS Handschar Division 1943-1945"*, Schiffer Military History, Atglen, PA, 1997.

Lucarelli Niccolò, *"Italiani in Albania 1939-1945"*, Delta Editrice, Parma, 2021.

Mattesini Francesco, *"La Decisione di Mussolini di Occupare la Grecia"*, Soldiershop Publishing, Zanica, 2020.

Montanari Mario, *"L'Esercito Italiano nella Campagna di Grecia"*, Ufficio Storico Stato Maggiore dell'Esercito, Rome, 1999.

Ruka Shahin, Dingu Kadri, Mullisi Nikolla, *"Tirana e aksioneve dhe barrikadave 1939-1944"*, Arian, Tiranë, 2003.

Smiley David, *"Albanian Assignment"*, Chatto & Windus – The Hogarth Press, London, 1984.

Stato Maggiore Regio Esercito, *"Per te, Soldato d'Albania/Për Ty, Ushtar i Shqipnis"*, Rome, 1941.

Thomas Nigel, Abbott Peter, *"Partisan Warfare 1941-45"*, Osprey Publishing, Oxford, 1983.

Trani Silvia, *"L'Unione fra l'Italia e l'Albania. Censimento delle fonti (1939-1945) conservate negli archivi pubblici e privati di Roma"*, Ministero per i Beni e le Attività Culturali, Direzione Generale per gli Archivi, Rome, 2007.

Zaugg Franziska A., *"Albanische Muslime in der Waffen-SS: Von Großalbanien zur Division Skanderbeg"*, Ferdinand Schöningh Verlag, Paderborn, 2016.

TITOLI GIÀ PUBBLICATI - TITLES ALREADY PUBLISHING

www.ingramcontent.com/pod-product-compliance
Lightning Source LLC
LaVergne TN
LVHW070522070526
838199LV00072B/6681